Prompt

A short guide to masterful AI prompting

Library of Canada Cataloguing in Publication data is available.
ISBN 978-1-989528-39-6 (Paperback Edition)
ISBN 978-1-989528-40-2 (E-book Edition)
ISBN 978-1-989528-41-9 (Digital Edition)

First Edition Printing 2024

Edited by Sarah Hook Nilsson
Book design by Soraya De Oliveira Reis

Published in Canada by Above the Noise, New Glasgow, NS
www.abovethenoisepublishing.com.

For more information contact: publishing@abovethenoise.ca
Special discounts are available on quantity purchases by corporations, associations, and others. For details, contact the publisher at the address above.

For more information on the book and author please visit www.aaronbethune.com

To those who seek clarity in their questions and courage in their answers.

And to the storytellers—whether through words, actions, or silent persistence—who remind us that our voices matter.

This book is for you.

Contents

The Seeker and the Power of Prompts

In a distant kingdom surrounded by jagged, snow-capped mountains, there was a young scholar named Kael. Known for his insatiable curiosity and relentless determination, Kael sought knowledge that surpassed even the greatest libraries of the land. Rumour spoke of a sage who lived in a cave high in the mountains, a keeper of wisdom so profound that a single conversation could change one's fate.

Many had tried to reach the sage, but the path was treacherous. The mountain winds howled like wolves, and the cliffs were sharp and unforgiving. Yet, Kael's heart was determined, and he believed that understanding the art of asking the right question was the true key to unlocking any mystery.

Kael packed his gear and set out at dawn. After two days of arduous climbing, he had made headway and got higher on the mountain. By now icy gusts lashed at his face, and loose stones threatened his every step; he recalled the advice of his mentor, a retired explorer named Thorne.

"Kael," Thorne had said, "a question is like a torch in the dark. Shine it poorly, and you'll see shadows and half-truths. But direct it well, and you'll find your way to the heart of any answer."

After the third day of perilous climbing, Kael finally reached the mouth of the cave. It was dark and silent, save for the steady drip of melting icicles. Within, the sage sat cross-legged, his eyes closed.

"Why have you come, seeker?" the sage asked as if expecting him, his voice deep and resonant.

Kael's heart pounded. He knew many before him had come seeking wealth, power, or simple answers, only to leave empty-handed and bewildered. Taking a deep breath, Kael remembered Thorne's words and chose his question with care.

"Sage," he said, "I seek not gold or glory but the wisdom to ask the questions that reveal true understanding. How does one craft a question that opens the doors to insight?"

The sage's eyes opened, and a glimmer of approval shone within them.

"You seek the essence of wisdom," the sage replied. "The power of a question lies not in its demand but in its invitation. A great question is precise yet open, guiding yet curious. To craft such a question is to wield the light that pierces the unknown."

The cave seemed to hum with energy as the sage spoke. Kael felt a warmth spreading through him, as if he was being filled with light.

"Remember," the sage continued, "when you seek knowledge, shape your question to illuminate the path, not just the destination."

Kael nodded, a newfound clarity taking root in his mind. The journey down the mountain was no easier, but each step felt lighter, charged with purpose. When he returned to the kingdom, Thorne met him with a proud smile.

"What did you learn, Kael?" Thorne asked.

Kael's eyes shone. "I learned that the true power is not in the answer itself, but in the question that guides you there."

Thorne clapped a hand on his shoulder. "Then you hold the key to unlocking every mystery you will face."

And so, Kael shared this wisdom with others, teaching them not just to seek answers but to ask questions that revealed the deepest truths.

Introduction

Welcome to a journey into the art and power of prompts. This book is designed to help you think differently about how you interact with AI tools, especially those that respond to prompts and questions. While it may seem that the quality of a response depends solely on the tool, the truth is that it is profoundly influenced by how you craft your prompts.

The purpose of this book is simple: to empower you to become a power user of AI by understanding that the tool gets better with the knowledge and creativity of the user. Prompts are not just questions; they are the keys to unlocking insights, fostering creativity, and guiding AI to become a true partner in your endeavors. By learning to create thoughtful and precise prompts, you will find that AI can enhance your knowledge, augment your capabilities, and spark new ideas—without replacing your unique intuition and expertise.

In these pages, you will discover practical techniques, common mistakes to avoid, and advanced strategies for refining your prompting skills. Whether you are a seasoned professional looking to leverage AI in your work or a curious learner wanting to deepen your understanding, this short book will guide you toward more effective and meaningful interactions with AI.

Let this book be your guide not only to asking better questions, but also becoming an empowered and intuitive user who collaborates seamlessly with AI, shaping technology to serve your creative and intellectual pursuits.

Why Me?

My journey has taken me through a wide range of experiences that have prepared me to guide you in mastering the art of prompting and storytelling. As a journalist, I spent years interviewing musicians, celebrities, and influential leaders, learning firsthand how powerful questions can unlock stories and reveal truths. I became skilled at asking the right questions—those that sparked deep, meaningful conversations and unearthed insights that might otherwise have remained hidden.

Hosting my podcast gave me an even greater appreciation for the nuances of dialogue and storytelling. I spoke with authors, industry pioneers, and thought leaders, further honing my ability to navigate conversations that not only entertained, but informed and inspired.

Beyond media, I have had the privilege of helping countless clients craft and share their stories.

Working with authors to shape their books taught me the importance of asking questions that draw out the most compelling narratives. Through coaching and collaboration, I've witnessed firsthand how powerful it is to turn raw experience into stories that resonate and create change.

My work doesn't stop at storytelling—I've co-founded AI startups where I blended my passion for narrative with cutting-edge technology. This experience has equipped me to bridge the gap between human intuition and AI's potential, creating tools that help people express their voices with more power and precision. These ventures have given me unique insight into how technology can be harnessed to enhance, not replace, our innate ability to communicate and connect.

Drawing from these experiences—journalist, podcast host, co-author, coach, and tech innovator—I'm in a unique position to show you how to craft prompts that not only work but elevate your communication and impact. This book is a culmination of everything I've learned about uncovering core stories and aligning them with purpose, helping you harness the power of AI to amplify your voice and connect with others in meaningful ways.

What is ChatGPT?

ChatGPT is an advanced language model developed by OpenAI, trained on a vast dataset to understand and generate human-like text. At its core, it operates using a type of artificial intelligence known as a transformer model. This architecture enables it to process text inputs, break them down into smaller units called tokens, and predict subsequent words to generate coherent responses.

Example:

- **Tokenization:** ChatGPT breaks down the phrase "ChatGPT is an AI model" into tokens: ['Chat', 'GPT', 'is', 'an', 'AI', 'model'].
- **Prediction:** The model uses these tokens to predict the most probable next words based on the input and its training.

When interacting with ChatGPT and employing prompt engineering, think of the process as being akin to *guiding a skilled but literal-minded apprentice*. The AI has vast knowledge and capabilities, but it depends entirely on how well you instruct it. Your prompts act as the blueprint for the response, so clarity, detail, and structure are crucial to getting the desired outcome.

Picture ChatGPT as a flashlight in a dark room filled with information. Your prompts determine where the flashlight points and how brightly it shines. A vague prompt is like loosely waving the flashlight around—it might illuminate something useful, but it could miss key details. A well-crafted prompt is like focusing the beam precisely where you want, revealing exactly what you need. The more context and direction you give, the sharper and more relevant the light's focus becomes. The flashlight's ability to light your way depends on you.

Approach your interactions with intentionality, ensuring that your prompts provide the right level of detail and context to guide ChatGPT effectively.

Treat your conversation not as static question-and-answer exchanges but as evolving dialogues. Adjust and refine your prompts like an experienced explorer who learns with each step. Begin with broader inquiries to establish the terrain, then narrow your focus for depth and precision. Recognize that each prompt isn't just a command but an ongoing adjustment to your path in the dark room. By thinking of each interaction as a part of an unfolding narrative, you guide the conversation strategically, ensuring that your literal-minded apprentice (ChatGPT) reveals not just what's asked, but what's most valuable along the way.

The key is continuous adaptation: listen to what ChatGPT reveals, fine-tune your prompts, and lead it toward the insights and responses that align best with your goals.

Why Prompt Quality Matters

A well-crafted prompt can make the difference between receiving an insightful response and a generic or confusing one. Prompts that are too vague may result in responses that lack depth or relevance. Conversely, a well-structured prompt provides clear direction and context.

Quality prompts also help AI responses align with your specific needs, capturing nuances that a general prompt might miss. By choosing words that clarify the desired tone, depth, or focus, you guide the AI to deliver results that are not only relevant but also tailored to your audience, purpose, or objective. In short, investing time in crafting a precise prompt enhances both efficiency and the value of the response, leading to outcomes that feel personalized, actionable, and aligned with your goals.

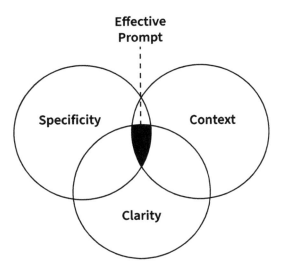

Key Principles: Specificity, Context, and Clarity

Principle 1: Specificity

Specific prompts guide the AI to focus on relevant aspects of a topic. For instance, instead of asking, "What is the history of Ancient Greece?", you could ask, "Provide an overview of the significant historical events in ancient Greece from 500 BC to 300 BC."

Principle 2: Context

Adding context helps the AI tailor its response. For example, if you need an article summary, specify its intended use: "Summarize this article for a beginner-level audience interested in environmental science."

Principle 3: Clarity

Clear prompts avoid ambiguity. For instance, "What is photosynthesis in plants" is clearer than "Explain it."

Example:

*   **Vague Prompt:** "Tell me about dogs."

    Output: General information on dogs.

*   **Detailed Prompt:** "Explain the different breeds of dogs that are well-suited for families with children, highlighting their temperaments and care needs."

Output: A detailed response focusing on breeds such as Labrador Retrievers, Golden Retrievers, and Beagles with relevant details on each.

The Power of Words and Word Choices in Masterful Prompts

Words are not just tools; they are the architects of thought and understanding. In crafting masterful prompts, every word chosen holds the potential to shape the direction, depth, and relevance of the response. The right word can open up pathways to profound insight, while an imprecise one can lead to confusion or incomplete answers.

Precision in Word Choice

Selecting the right words is akin to sharpening a blade. A prompt must be as precise as possible, conveying exactly what you want to uncover. For example, compare these two prompts:

- Vague: "Tell me about medical technology."

- Precise: "Explain how artificial intelligence is transforming the healthcare industry, focusing on patient diagnosis and treatment."

The precise prompt not only specifies the technology but also narrows the context to an industry and two key aspects, guiding the response to a more meaningful and comprehensive answer.

Impactful and Contextual Words

The context set by a prompt can determine the breadth or focus of the response. Words like "explain," "summarize," "compare," or "analyze" create clear expectations for the type of response desired.

- "Explain" invites detailed descriptions and background.

- "Summarize" calls for concise overviews.

- "Compare" sets up responses that highlight similarities and differences.

- "Analyze" prompts a deeper examination, breaking down components, identifying causes and effects, or exploring underlying factors.

Evocative Language for Open Exploration

When seeking creative or exploratory answers, using words that evoke curiosity and wonder can enhance the response. For instance, beginning a prompt with "Imagine," "What if," or "Describe a scenario where" encourages responses that explore beyond the conventional.

Example:

"Imagine a world where humans and AI coexist harmoniously. What would that society look like?"

Crafting Questions with Balance

A masterful prompt balances precision with openness, allowing for comprehensive answers while staying relevant. The right prompt doesn't restrict, but it directs; it doesn't command, but it leads.

Understanding the power of word choices helps prompt engineers to create queries that reveal the fullest depth of knowledge and insight, guiding not only the response but the path of discovery itself.

The Importance of One's Own Knowledge

While the art of prompt crafting can unlock significant insights, the asker's own knowledge of the topic plays a crucial role in shaping effective questions. The deeper one's understanding, the more refined and specific one's prompts can become, which in turn leads to more meaningful and accurate responses.

Enhancing Prompt Quality with Prior Knowledge

When someone has a solid grasp of the topic, they can:

- Identify relevant details to include in prompts.

- Recognize the nuances that may guide the AI toward more targeted responses.

- Frame questions that go beyond surface-level inquiries, leading to richer and more comprehensive answers.

For example, someone with a basic understanding of climate change might ask, "What are the effects of global warming?", while a more knowledgeable person could refine the question to, "What specific strategies are being implemented in Europe to mitigate the impact of global warming on coastal cities?"

Guiding AI with Informed Context

The more you know about a subject, the better you can shape prompts that guide AI toward relevant and insightful answers. Informed context allows for:

- Anticipating possible answers and structuring follow-up questions.
- Evaluating the quality and depth of the AI's responses, ensuring that they meet the desired level of expertise.
- Using terminology and references that align with expert discourse, which signals to the AI to respond in kind.

Building on AI Responses

Even when the initial response from the AI is helpful, a well-informed user can iterate on the prompt to explore deeper angles. For instance, if an AI response to a prompt about the benefits of renewable energy is too general, knowledge of specific technologies like wind or solar power enables the user to refine their query: "Can you compare the energy output efficiency of offshore wind turbines to traditional solar panels?"

In essence, the asker's own understanding acts as a catalyst for unlocking the full potential of AI. It empowers them to craft prompts that do more than seek answers; they drive conversations that reveal deeper truths and connections.

AI Limitations and Setting Realistic Expectations

Understanding the limitations of AI helps set realistic expectations and enhances your ability to use it effectively.

Recognizing AI Boundaries

AI is powerful but not infallible. It can lack up-to-date knowledge, struggle with subjective judgments, and misinterpret complex context.

Tip: Double-check AI-generated information, especially when accuracy is critical, such as in technical writing or academic work.

Setting Realistic Goals

While AI can generate insightful and creative content, it may not always provide perfect or complete solutions. Knowing when to use it as an aid rather than a primary source is key.

- **Example:** Use AI to brainstorm ideas or draft outlines, but rely on your expertise for final edits and fact-checking.

Combining Human Insight

AI works best when paired with human judgment. Your knowledge and critical thinking can guide the AI's output toward more useful and meaningful results.

How to Evaluate AI Responses

Evaluating Depth and Clarity

When evaluating AI responses, ensure that the content is not only relevant but sufficiently detailed to meet your expectations. Consider whether the response addresses your main points and if any important aspects are left unexplored.

1. Evaluate Clarity and Cohesion

- **Ask Yourself:** Is the response logically structured and easy to understand? If it feels disjointed or unclear, refine your prompt to request more organization or examples.

- **Example:** If your response feels fragmented, a follow-up like "Can you provide a structured explanation with examples?" can help guide the AI to produce more coherent content.

2. Check for Accuracy

AI models rely on their training data, which might not always be current or fully correct. Double-check facts, figures, or detailed claims against reliable sources to ensure accuracy .

Tip: If using AI for specialized or professional work, validate the content with an expert or trusted source.

3. Iterating on Feedback

Use the responses as a starting point for further inquiry. If the answer isn't quite right, rephrase or add more context to your prompt. The process of refinement can often lead to richer and more complete answers.

Example Iterative Process:

- Initial prompt: "Tell me about renewable energy."
- Follow-up: "Can you focus on how renewable energy impacts urban development?"
- Additional query: "Explain the challenges cities face when integrating solar and wind energy."

By iterating this way, you guide the conversation toward deeper and more relevant insights.

The Power of Creativity and Intuition in Prompting

While precision and structure are essential for effective prompting, creativity and intuition elevate the process from functional to exceptional. By blending structured thinking with imaginative approaches, you can craft prompts that lead to unexpected insights, unique perspectives, and engaging interactions.

Why Creativity Matters

Creativity allows you to think outside the box and approach problems from different angles. It's particularly valuable when:

- **Exploring New Ideas:** When brainstorming, creative prompts can spark unique outputs that conventional questions might not elicit.

- **Driving Engagement:** Creative prompts make interactions more dynamic and open-ended, encouraging exploration and conversation.

Examples of Creative Prompts

Instead of asking, "What are the benefits of remote work?" consider a prompt like, "Imagine a future where remote work is the global norm. How might this reshape urban living and societal norms?"

To delve into historical analysis, rather than asking, "Explain the causes of World War II," you could prompt, "If social media had existed during the lead-up to World War II, how might it have changed public sentiment and international relations?"

Harnessing Intuition in Prompting

Intuition, built from experience and knowledge, helps you sense the direction a prompt should take for maximum impact. It guides you in choosing:

- **Which Details to Include:** Knowing when to add context or let a prompt remain open-ended.
- **How to Frame Follow-Ups:** Recognizing when a follow-up should deepen a topic or pivot to a related issue.

Combining Creativity and Structure

The most effective prompts combine the creativity of exploration with the structure of targeted inquiry. For example:

- Creative angle: "Describe how an AI might narrate the story of humanity if it were the sole witness to our history."

- Structured directive: "Ensure your response highlights key technological milestones and cultural shifts."

Tips for Cultivating Creativity in Prompting

- **Use Analogies and Scenarios:** Frame prompts with metaphors or hypothetical situations to draw out richer responses. For instance, "If renewable energy were a new type of currency, how would it influence global economics?"

- **Experiment with Word Choices:** Use action-oriented and evocative language like "envision," "hypothesize," or "reimagine" to open up responses.

- **Balance Open-Ended and Focused Approaches:** Blend prompts that encourage free-form creativity with those that steer the conversation, ensuring responses remain relevant.

In summary, incorporating creativity and intuition into your prompt strategy can transform your interactions from basic inquiries into engaging dialogues that expand knowledge and foster new ideas.

The Continuing Conversation: Iterating After the Initial Prompt

Crafting a powerful initial prompt is only the beginning. To harness the full potential of an AI interaction, one must view the process as an ongoing dialogue. A single prompt may open the door, but it is the follow-up questions and iterative exchanges that lead to deeper insights and richer understanding.

Adding Depth and Practical Techniques

1. Types of Follow-Up Questions

To ensure a more comprehensive dialogue, consider different types of follow-up questions:

- **Clarifying Questions:** Ask for more details or a clearer explanation (e.g., "What are the main challenges hospitals face when implementing AI for diagnostics?").

- **Probing Questions:** Encourage deeper exploration of a specific aspect (e.g., "How do these diagnostic improvements impact patient outcomes over the long term?").

- **Comparative Questions:** Request a comparison between different factors (e.g., "How does the use of AI in diagnostic accuracy compare between large metropolitan hospitals and smaller, rural ones?").

2. Techniques for Refining Prompts

Iterative prompting involves refining your questions based on the AI's previous responses. Here's how to do it effectively:

- **Assess Gaps:** Identify any missing details or areas where the response was insufficient. Use targeted follow-ups to fill these gaps.

- **Reframe for Clarity:** If the initial response is unclear, rephrase your follow-up for better precision (e.g., "Can you break down that answer into the main pros and cons?").

- **Layering Questions:** Build upon each response by layering questions that gradually increase in complexity (e.g., start with "What technologies are used?" and follow with "Which of these technologies have the most potential for future development?").

3. Keeping the Conversation Focused

It's easy for an AI interaction to become too broad or lose focus. To maintain a clear direction:

- **Set Parameters:** Include specific constraints in your follow-ups (e.g., "Within the context of diagnostic AI, what role do algorithms play in detecting rare diseases?").

- **Redirect When Necessary:** If the conversation veers off course, use a guiding question to steer it back (e.g., "Let's focus on how AI impacts patient care directly. Can you elaborate on that?").

4. Encouraging Comprehensive Answers

To obtain more holistic responses:

- **Prompt for Multiple Perspectives:** Ask the AI to provide different viewpoints or stakeholder opinions (e.g., "What are the perspectives of patients versus doctors on the use of AI in diagnostics?").

- **Request Examples and Data:** Encourage the AI to include examples, data points, or case studies for support (e.g., "Can you give a specific case where AI led to a significant breakthrough in diagnostic accuracy?").

When to Start a New Conversation and Begin Fresh

In your interactions with AI, there are times when it's best to reset and start a new conversation instead of continuing the current thread. Starting fresh can ensure clarity, relevancy, and better alignment with your new goals.

Signs It's Time to Start Over:

1. **Topic Shift:** If your questions start diverging significantly from the original subject, starting a

new conversation helps reset context and focus.

2. **Response Degradation:** If the AI's responses become less relevant or stray from your desired depth, it may be pulling too much context from prior interactions.

3. **Complexity Build-Up:** Conversations that involve numerous follow-up prompts can accumulate context that skews responses. Resetting ensures that only your new question directs the output.

4. **Change of Intent:** When switching from exploration (e.g., brainstorming) to structured tasks (e.g., generating an outline), it's beneficial to start anew for the AI to better understand the shift.

Benefits of a New Start:

- **Fresh Context:** The AI can refocus solely on your current query without potential confusion from previous exchanges.

- **Improved Precision:** Prompts are answered based on clear, isolated context, leading to more accurate responses.

- **Cleaner Slate for Follow-Ups:** Establishing new ground allows for better targeted follow-up questions aligned with your new intent.

By recognizing when to refresh your approach, you'll maximize the effectiveness of your interactions and ensure you receive high-quality, contextually accurate answers.

Common Mistakes and How to Avoid Them

Crafting prompts is an art that requires practice. While there are many ways to create effective prompts, there are also common pitfalls that can hinder the quality of responses. Being aware of these mistakes can help you refine your technique and avoid frustration.

1. **Vague or Broad Prompts**

- **Mistake**: Asking questions that are too general, such as "Tell me something about the history of the Renaissance," often leads to responses that lack depth and relevance.

- **Solution**: Add specificity and focus. For example, refine the prompt to "Summarize the major events of European history during the Renaissance period."

2. **Overloading the Prompt**

- **Mistake**: Combining too many questions or requests in a single prompt, like "Explain how AI works and its benefits, and tell me about its risks and future trends."
- **Solution**: Break down complex prompts into separate, focused queries to ensure clarity and detailed answers.

3. **Ambiguous Language**

- **Mistake**: Using vague words or phrases that can be interpreted in multiple ways, leading to unclear responses.
- **Solution**: Use precise language and avoid ambiguous terms. Instead of saying "Tell me about green energy tech," specify "Discuss the latest advancements in renewable energy technology."

4. **Lack of Context**

- **Mistake**: Failing to provide background information or context that could guide the response in the right direction.

- **Solution**: Frame the prompt with enough context. For example, rather than asking, "What are some leadership skills?" specify, "What leadership skills are most valuable for managing remote teams?"

5. **Expecting Too Much from a Single Prompt**

- **Mistake**: Believing one prompt can yield exhaustive answers on complex topics.
- **Solution**: Recognize the value of follow-up questions and iterative prompting to build on initial responses and explore deeper insights.

Memory-Aware Prompting

Think of memory in AI as digital continuity in which the system retains details across sessions, making interactions feel seamless and personalized. When active, ChatGPT's memory can recall specific details for future sessions, such as project goals, preferred communication style, or character elements in a story.

Imagine speaking with a colleague who remembers details from your last conversation, even if it was weeks ago. Memory enables ChatGPT to provide that same level of familiarity and relevance, enriching your experience by minimizing the need to repeat foundational information.

Why Memory Matters in Prompting

Effective prompting already allows for precise, insightful responses, but memory can take this further by preserving details, context, and preferences. Memory helps:

- **Build Context Over Time**: Just as you wouldn't start from scratch every time you meet with a trusted partner, memory lets you continue conversations without reiterating background information.

- **Enhance Personalization**: By remembering your preferences and nuances, ChatGPT can tailor responses in ways that reflect your style, tone, and objectives.

- **Boost Efficiency**: With memory, you save time on re-establishing context, allowing each session to build naturally on the last.

When used thoughtfully, memory helps ChatGPT evolve from a reactive tool into a more proactive, collaborative partner in your projects.

Techniques for Memory-Aware Prompting

To maximize the benefits of memory, here are specific prompting techniques that guide ChatGPT to use memory effectively.

Technique 1:
Setting Up Context to be Remembered

- *Prompt Example*: "For our future sessions, remember that this book project is targeted at young adults and should maintain a conversational tone. We're focusing on themes of resilience and self-discovery."

- *Explanation*: This prompt lays out specific details for memory, helping ChatGPT sustain the tone, audience focus, and thematic elements without needing constant reminders.

Technique 2:
Reinforcing Important Details

- *Prompt Example*: "Keep in mind that in this story,

the protagonist has a background in medicine, which affects their perspective on life. Let's maintain that in each chapter."

- *Explanation*: Repeating essential points occasionally helps reinforce ChatGPT's memory of these elements, making the responses more consistent over time.

Technique 3:
Overriding or Updating Memory

- *Prompt Example*: "Forget our previous discussions about setting the story in a rural area; let's focus on an urban setting now."

- *Explanation*: This prompt directs ChatGPT to adjust its memory, making way for new information that better aligns with your evolving project needs.

Technique 4:
Leveraging Memory for Layered Context

- *Prompt Example*: "Remember that the protagonist's relationship with their sibling is strained due to past conflicts, and this will influence their actions moving forward."

- *Explanation*: This layered memory helps ChatGPT maintain consistency, making it easier for you to build complex, interwoven storylines or projects without rehashing background information.

Aplications of Memory in Professional and Creative Fields

Let's explore some practical examples where memory can significantly enhance the user experience across different domains:

- **Project Management**: Imagine working on a business project over multiple sessions. Memory enables ChatGPT to recall your project's goals, your preferred style of communication, and any relevant client-specific information.

    Example:

    "Remember that our project focuses on sustainable practices in the fashion industry. We're targeting insights for eco-conscious designers."

- **Educational Tutoring**: Teachers or tutors can use memory to help ChatGPT recall a student's progress, strengths, and areas needing improvement, facilitating a more effective and personalized learning journey.

Example:

"Please remember that my student struggles with algebra but excels in geometry. Let's focus our next sessions on simplifying algebra concepts."

- **Creative Writing**: Authors can benefit immensely from ChatGPT's memory for character details, plot twists, or stylistic elements, allowing for a richer, more cohesive story development process.

  Example:

  "Keep in mind that the protagonist's underlying motivation is fear of failure, which influences their decisions. Let's make sure that stays consistent in upcoming chapters."

- **Marketing and Brand Development**: Memory can assist in maintaining a consistent brand voice, especially when developing long-term marketing materials or strategies.

  Example:

  "Please remember our brand voice is warm, optimistic, and customer-focused. We're targeting young adults who value sustainability."

Considerations and Limitations of Memory in Prompting

While memory is powerful, it's also essential to be mindful of its current limitations:

- **Incompleteness**: ChatGPT's memory may not retain every detail perfectly. For complex projects, it's helpful to refresh ChatGPT on key points occasionally.

- **Relevance**: If a project's direction shifts, it's crucial to guide ChatGPT in letting go of outdated information.

    Example:

    Explicitly stating, "Let's disregard previous marketing strategies and focus on a new campaign angle," helps streamline memory.

- **Privacy Concerns**: Be aware of any sensitive information stored in memory. Although ChatGPT's memory can be cleared, exercising caution with confidential details is always prudent.

Ethical Use of Memory and Privacy Considerations

Using memory responsibly is key to fostering trust and security. Here are a few tips to ensure ethical memory use:

- **Transparency**: Be clear about what information you're comfortable having stored in memory. Regularly reviewing what ChatGPT remembers can help maintain transparency.

- **Data Management**: For sensitive projects, it's a good idea to prompt ChatGPT to forget certain details once they're no longer needed.

- **Consent in Collaborative Settings**: When using ChatGPT for team projects, ensure all members are comfortable with memory usage and any stored details.

With well-crafted prompts, you can guide ChatGPT to retain relevant details, adapt to evolving contexts, and support complex, ongoing projects. By embracing memory-aware prompting, you're not just asking questions but building a rich, dynamic relationship with AI that evolves and grows with your needs.

Advanced Techniques for Complex Queries

When delving into complex or multifaceted questions, employing advanced prompt strategies can help. Here are some techniques to enhance responses:

Layering Prompts

Layering involves breaking down a complex query into steps and asking the AI to build on previous answers. Start with a foundational question and use follow-ups to add detail and depth.

Example:

- Initial prompt: "Explain the effects of climate change on global agriculture."
- Follow-up: "Can you break down the impact on specific crops like rice, wheat, and maize?"

Conditional Prompts

Use conditional language to guide responses based on specific criteria. This helps tailor answers to different scenarios.

- **Example**: "If the company adopts renewable energy sources, describe the potential cost savings. If not, outline the likely long-term financial risks."

Chaining Responses

For a comprehensive exploration, you can create a chain of prompts that progressively deepen the discussion. This approach is useful for research or in-depth writing.

Example:

"Provide an overview of recent AI advancements. Next, analyze the social implications of these developments, focusing on job displacement."

Using Conditional and Comparative Prompts

Guiding AI with If/Then Logic Conditional prompts help direct the AI's focus based on potential input scenarios. For example: "If the input is a positive number, explain its mathematical properties. If not, explain why it isn't."

Example:

*   **Prompt**: "If the year is before 1900, provide significant historical events. If the year is after 1900, focus on technological advancements."
*   **Expected Output**: A differentiated response based on the specified conditions.

Using Linked and Multi-Part Prompts

To gain detailed, layered insights, combine multiple questions or link them in a single prompt. For example: "Explain the benefits of renewable energy. Then, compare solar and wind energy based on cost-effectiveness."

Example:

*   **Prompt**: "Describe the health benefits of meditation, and then outline a 7-day beginner meditation plan."

- **Expected Output**: A response that first covers general health benefits, followed by a step-by-step plan.

Ethical Considerations in Prompting

Prompt engineering is powerful, but with great power comes responsibility. Understanding the ethical implications of prompting ensures that interactions are constructive and considerate.

Avoiding Bias

AI responses can reflect biases present in the training data. Craft your prompts in a way that minimizes leading language or loaded terms.

 Tip: Use neutral and inclusive language. Instead of "Why is X better than Y?" consider "Compare the benefits and drawbacks of X and Y."

Promoting Constructive Use

Ensure your prompts encourage positive, productive, or educational interactions. Avoid prompts that could be used to generate misleading or harmful content.

Transparency and Accountability

Be clear about your intentions when using AI to create content, especially if it will be shared publicly. Crediting AI contributions can foster transparency.

Developing Efficient Prompt Templates

Creating reusable templates for common tasks saves time and ensures consistency in your responses. For example, a product description template might be: "Write a [tone: enthusiastic/professional] description for [product name], focusing on [key features] and ending with a call to action."

To make these templates even more powerful:

Customize for Specific Audiences

Tailor the language or focus points based on the target audience. For instance, a description for tech enthusiasts might include more technical details, while a general consumer version should emphasize ease of use and benefits.

Include Variables for Easy Adaptation

Identify placeholders, such as [product name], [key features], and [tone], that you can quickly swap to fit different products or contexts.

Test and Refine

Use the templates in practice and tweak them based on the responses you receive. If certain phrasings yield better results, update the template accordingly.

Add Specifics for Clarity

Include guidance on word count, format (e.g., bullet points or paragraph), or additional elements such as testimonials or use cases, if needed. For example,

"Write a [100-150 word, bullet-point] description for [product name], emphasizing [benefits and unique selling points]."

By developing and refining a set of efficient templates, you create a toolkit that can streamline your workflow and improve the quality and consistency of your outputs.

Checklist for Effective Prompting and Iterative Conversations

Use this checklist to guide your prompting and iterative interactions with AI, ensuring each exchange is as productive and insightful as possible.

Before You Start:

1. **Clarify Your Objective**

     ☐   What is the goal of your interaction? (e.g., gathering information, generating ideas, solving a problem)

2. **Assess Your Knowledge**

   ☐ Do you have enough background on the topic to frame a meaningful prompt?

3. **Choose Your Approach**

   ☐ Will this be a precise query or an open-ended question for exploration?

Crafting Your Initial Prompt:

4. **Be Specific and Clear**

   ☐ Is your prompt detailed enough to guide the AI? (e.g., "Explain how AI impacts patient diagnosis" vs "Tell me about the use of AI in healthcare")

5. **Use Powerful Keywords**

   ☐ Have you included words that set the context? (e.g., explain, compare, analyze)

6. **Set Parameters (If Needed)**

   ☐ Does your prompt include necessary constraints? (e.g., "Explain the impact of AI in healthcare, focusing on diagnosis")

Iterating After the Initial Prompt:

7. **Review the Initial Response**
   - ☐ Does the response align with your expectations?
   - ☐ Are there areas lacking detail or clarity?

8. **Formulate Follow-Up Questions**
   - ☐ What clarifying or probing questions can you ask?
     (e.g., "Can you provide examples?")

9. **Layer Questions for Depth**
   - ☐ Have you planned questions that build on previous answers?

10. **Check for Completeness**
    - ☐ Does the response cover all aspects of your initial query?
    - ☐ If not, ask for additional details
      (e.g., "What challenges are associated with this?")

Enhancing the Quality of Responses:

11. **Refine Your Prompts**
    - ☐ If the response is too broad or vague, how can you rephrase the question for better focus?

12. **Direct the AI When Needed**
    - ☐ Use guiding questions to maintain a clear direction (e.g., "Let's focus on patient outcomes. Can you expand on that?")

13. **Ask for Supporting Data**
    - ☐ Have you requested examples or case studies for more context?

Final Steps:

14. **Evaluate Relevance and Accuracy**
    - ☐ Does the answer match the scope of your inquiry? Is it factually accurate?

15. **Incorporate Your Knowledge**
    - ☐ Does the response align with what you know? Can your expertise refine the interaction further?

16. **Repeat the Process**
    - ☐ Are there new questions or angles to explore based on the response?

Reflecting on the Interaction:

17. **Summarize Insights**
    - ☐ What key takeaways have you gathered?

18. **Identify Gaps**
    - ☐ Are there any unanswered questions that require additional prompts?

19. **Plan Your Next Steps**
    - ☐ Is further research needed? What follow-up questions can deepen your understanding?

Keep this checklist handy to make sure you approach each prompt with confidence and strategic thinking, turning every AI interaction into an opportunity for meaningful discovery and insight.

Final Thoughts

Kael's journey up the treacherous mountain to seek wisdom from the sage was more than just a quest for answers; it was a testament to the power of asking the right questions and persevering through the process of discovery. Just as Kael learned that the strength of a question shapes the path to knowledge, so too you can harness this understanding in your interactions with AI.

Crafting prompts is not merely about posing questions but about creating a dialogue where your input shapes the output. It is an iterative process, where each response invites new prompts, clarifies understanding, and builds richer, more nuanced insights. Like Kael's climb, your journey with prompting is one of growth, exploration, and the continual refinement of your approach.

Remember AI is a tool that enhances, not replaces, your knowledge. The more you engage with it thoughtfully, the more it will complement your expertise and intuition.

As you continue to develop your prompting skills, keep these key lessons in mind:

- **Start with Purpose**: Every prompt should have a clear objective, much like Kael's carefully chosen question that unlocked the sage's wisdom.

- **Iterate for Insight**: Treat each response as a step along the path. Follow up, refine, and adapt as needed to illuminate your way forward.

- **Use Your Knowledge**: Bring your background and understanding into each prompt to guide the AI effectively, making it a true partner in discovery.

- **Embrace Creativity**: Don't be afraid to explore new angles and approaches, just as Kael's courage allowed him to reach the summit and gain deeper insight.

Now that you've journeyed through the principles and techniques of effective prompting, it's time to put what you've learned into practice. Start your own climb by revisiting past prompts, enhancing them with newfound precision and creativity. Experiment, iterate, and refine your approach as Kael did, learning with each step.

Challenge yourself to move beyond basic questions and seek out deeper, more meaningful interactions with AI. Treat your prompts as the guiding torches that light the way to knowledge, innovation, and creativity.

Kael returned from the mountain not with a single answer but with the understanding that great questions open doors to endless possibilities. You now have that same key. Use it to unlock insights, explore uncharted territories of thought, and elevate your interactions with AI. **The adventure begins with your next prompt—what will you ask?**

Author's Note

A book called *Prompt*, focused on the art of prompting, would fall short if I hadn't applied the very skills it explores in writing it. In creating this book, I've drawn on my expertise in prompt engineering, my background as a lifelong question-asker, and my deep curiosity about the possibilities of AI. I've applied my understanding of the subject, shaped by personal beliefs and approaches, to craft each chapter with intention. Just as I encourage readers to use prompts to unlock clarity, creativity, and purpose, I've used the same tools to bring this book to life. Thank you for joining me on this journey—I hope it inspires you to harness the power of your own prompts and, in doing so, transform how you communicate, create, and connect.

Prompts

At my company, *We Write Stories*, we offer a powerful AI tool called the MindTrust. A MindTrust is a secure vault of your accumulated knowledge, experiences, insights, expertise, communication style, stories, personality traits, intelligence type, thinking patterns, and personal data, unlocked and made accessible through AI.

The sample prompts that follow are designed to be general and applicable to a wide audience. However, for users of a MindTrust, the results are even more powerful. By leveraging your unique repository of knowledge and experiences, the AI can generate responses that are tailored to your specific context, ensuring that the advice and solutions are not only relevant but also aligned with your personal or organizational objectives.

If you're interested in harnessing the full potential of your knowledge and experiences through a MindTrust, I invite you to get in touch with us. Our team at *We Write Stories* is dedicated to helping you create a living repository that not only holds your wisdom but also communicates and thinks like you, enabling you to make a lasting impact. Visit *https://www.wewritestories.com/mind-trust* for *more information.*

Some of the following prompts require third-party collaborations and integrations. If you have a MindTrust they will work seamlessly. When in doubt, I recommend asking the AI directly how to improve or better implement a prompt. You will be amazed at how the AI can guide you to achieve the best results. If you want to learn more about ways to build AI into your workflow don't hesitate to get in touch.

Generating Articles

1. **Deep-Dive Analysis:**
   - "Write an article that analyzes the trends in [industry/topic] over the past decade. Present a balanced perspective that includes both my own professional insights and references to recent studies or reports."
   - *Example*: "Create an article analyzing the evolution of digital marketing strategies over the past 10 years. Include my observations as a seasoned marketer and relevant statistics."

2. **Comparative Pieces:**
   - "Draft an article comparing [two related concepts], focusing on their pros and cons from the perspective of a professional in [your field]. Highlight which option is better suited for specific scenarios."
   - *Example*: "Write an article comparing remote-first work culture versus hybrid work models, providing insights based on my experiences in organizational management."

3. **Exploring 'What If' Scenarios:**

- "Compose an article that explores the 'what if' scenario of [hypothetical situation], providing speculative yet informed insights based on my knowledge of [topic]."

- *Example*: "Write an article discussing what the future of content creation might look like if AI tools become the primary method of generating written content. Include potential challenges and opportunities."

Generating Newsletters

1. **Engagement-Focused Content:**

- "Create a newsletter issue that includes [topic or theme] and is structured to provide value through tips, insights, and a brief personal note that reflects my tone and connects with my audience."

- *Example*: "Draft a newsletter focused on productivity tips for creative professionals, sharing my favorite strategies and a short anecdote about how I applied them in my work."

2. **Industry Updates with Commentary:**

   - "Write a newsletter that curates the latest news in [specific field] and includes my expert commentary on why these updates matter and how they might impact readers."

   - *Example*: "Create a newsletter issue summarizing the latest changes in social media algorithms and providing my take on how businesses should adapt their content strategies."

3. **Personal Reflections and Insights:**

   - "Draft a newsletter that reflects on a recent project or trend I've encountered in [your field]. Share insights and lessons learned, inviting readers to engage or share their perspectives."

   - *Example*: "Write a newsletter discussing my experience with launching a new product feature and the unexpected challenges we faced. Include lessons learned and questions for readers about their product development journeys."

Crafting Marketing Campaigns

1. **Developing a Campaign Strategy:**

   - "Create a detailed outline for a marketing campaign that promotes [product/service] with a focus on [core value or unique selling point]. The campaign should reflect my tone of voice [e.g., enthusiastic, professional, empathetic] and resonate with [target audience]."

   - *Example*: "Design a marketing campaign for my new productivity app, emphasizing its ability to streamline workflow for busy professionals. Ensure the messaging is motivational and showcases real-life scenarios."

2. **Customer-Centric Messaging:**

   - "Draft a series of marketing messages that highlight the benefits of [product/service] from the perspective of [target demographic]. Each message should be crafted to evoke [e.g., excitement, trust, curiosity] and align with my voice as an [e.g., industry expert, relatable guide]."

- *Example*: "Create marketing content for a skincare line aimed at eco-conscious consumers, emphasizing sustainability and visible results with a caring, knowledgeable tone."

3. **Creating Themed Campaigns:**

   - "Outline a seasonal or event-based marketing campaign for [product/service] that aligns with my communication style of [e.g., witty, insightful, educational]. Include ideas for key messages and promotional hooks."

   - *Example*: "Plan a back-to-school marketing campaign for an educational platform, using an inspiring and informative tone that appeals to both students and parents."

Crafting Sales Emails

1. **Introductory Outreach:**

   - "Write a compelling introductory sales email for [product/service] that captures my communication style [describe your style, e.g., personable and informative]. The email should engage [target audience] and clearly convey how [product/service] solves their problem."

- *Example*: "Draft an introductory email for my project management software aimed at small business owners, using a conversational tone that highlights the benefits of simplified team collaboration."

2. **Follow-Up Emails:**

- "Create a follow-up sales email that references [previous interaction or offer] and reinforces the value of [product/service]. The tone should be [e.g., friendly, confident, reassuring] and encourage a positive response."

- *Example*: "Write a follow-up email for potential clients who attended my webinar, reminding them of the key takeaways and offering a special consultation package. Keep the tone professional yet warm."

3. **Promotional or Limited-Time Offers:**

- "Draft a sales email announcing a limited-time promotion for [product/service]. Ensure it reflects my [e.g., engaging, straightforward] communication style and motivates [target audience] to take immediate action."

- *Example*: "Create a promotional email for an online course with a 20% discount, emphasizing urgency and the unique benefits of signing up now. Keep the tone clear and persuasive."

Crafting Social Media Posts

1. **Educational or Insightful Posts:**
   - "Write a social media post for [platform, e.g., LinkedIn] that shares my expertise in [specific topic]. The tone should be [e.g., thought-provoking, educational] and encourage discussion among [target audience]."
   - *Example*: "Create a LinkedIn post explaining the top three trends in digital marketing for 2024 and what they mean for small business owners. Use an engaging, informative voice."

2. **Promotional Announcements:**
   - "Develop a social media post announcing [product/service launch, event, etc.]. The post should reflect my [e.g., lively, sincere] style and highlight key benefits to resonate with [target audience]."
   - *Example*: "Draft an Instagram post announcing the launch of a new sustainable fashion line, focusing on eco-friendly practices and

bold design. Use a tone that is both chic
and authentic."

3. **Engagement-Driven Content:**

    •   "Write a social media post that asks an
        engaging question related to [your field
        or topic], inviting [target audience] to share
        their thoughts. Keep the tone [e.g., approach-
        able, playful] to foster interaction."

    •   *Example*: "Create a Twitter post asking
        entrepreneurs, 'What's the most unexpected
        lesson you've learned from running your own
        business?' Use a relatable and conversational
        tone."

4. **Inspirational Content:**

    •   "Craft a motivational social media post that
        reflects my voice as [e.g., a mentor, industry
        leader] and speaks to [target audience] about
        overcoming challenges in [specific area]."

    •   *Example*: "Write a LinkedIn post sharing
        a short story about overcoming a major
        challenge in team leadership, and include a
        key takeaway that motivates others. Keep the
        tone authentic and uplifting."

Speech Preparation

1. **Retrieving Personal Stories:**

   - "List impactful personal stories from my career as a [your role] that align with the theme of [topic, e.g., innovation in the workplace]. Summarize each story in a way that highlights key lessons learned and relatable takeaways for the audience."

   - *Example*: "Find stories from my experience as a project manager that demonstrate overcoming major challenges with limited resources, and outline the main insights for a speech on resilience."

2. **Structuring a Keynote Address:**

   - "Outline a keynote speech on [specific topic], incorporating three key talking points that reflect my unique experiences and perspectives. Ensure that the content flows logically and includes an engaging introduction and conclusion."

   - *Example*: "Create a keynote outline on 'The Future of Remote Work,' using my expertise in HR management and including personal anecdotes that illustrate effective team strategies."

3. **Connecting with the Audience:**

- "Generate talking points for a speech on [topic] that include relatable analogies, personal experiences, and data-backed insights. Focus on connecting with [specific audience, e.g., young entrepreneurs] by using a [e.g., friendly, motivational] tone."

- *Example*: "Prepare talking points for a speech about leadership in startups, incorporating lessons I learned from launching my own business and data on successful leadership traits."

Panel Discussions

1. **Highlighting Expert Opinions:**

- "Prepare a list of key points I should mention when discussing [topic] in a panel setting. Include my unique viewpoints and relevant industry data that would be valuable to the conversation."

- *Example*: "Create a set of key points for a panel on the ethical use of AI, including my position as a technology consultant and insights into recent industry trends."

2. **Anticipating Audience Questions:**

- "Develop potential audience questions for a panel discussion on [topic], along with concise, informed responses based on my background and expertise."

- *Example*: "Predict questions for a panel on sustainable business practices, and provide sample responses that include my experience with green initiatives."

3. **Quick Reference Stories:**

- "Summarize short stories from my career that I can reference during a panel on [topic]. These stories should be adaptable for answering various questions or making points during the discussion."

- *Example*: "Find quick, adaptable stories about product development successes and challenges from my time at a tech startup for a panel on product innovation."

Interviews

1. **Preparing Insightful Answers:**
   - "Draft potential interview questions I might be asked about [specific topic], and provide well-rounded, insightful answers that reflect my knowledge and experiences."
   - *Example*: "Generate common interview questions about digital transformation, with responses that include my role in leading such changes within a corporate environment."

2. **Highlighting Key Achievements:**
   - "Create a list of my major professional achievements related to [topic] that I can mention during an interview. Include context and outcomes to make each one impactful."
   - *Example*: "Summarize my significant achievements in leading marketing campaigns that doubled client engagement for a media interview about successful strategies."

3. **Memorable Talking Points:**
   - "Develop three memorable talking points for an interview on [topic]. Each point should showcase my expertise and be framed in a

way that leaves a lasting impression."

- *Example*: "Draft three key points for an interview on work-life balance, incorporating my unique strategies for maintaining productivity and well-being."

Speech and Panel Engagements

1. **Storytelling for Engagement:**
   - "Choose two or three compelling stories from my past experiences that align with [specific topic]. Ensure that each story has a clear beginning, middle, and end, and includes a key takeaway relevant to the audience."
   - *Example*: "Select stories from my consulting career that showcase transformative moments in team management for a speech on effective leadership."

2. **Insights from Current Trends:**
   - "Summarize recent trends in [field/topic] and explain how I can use them to add timely and relevant insights during my upcoming speaking engagement."

- *Example*: "Summarize the latest trends in cybersecurity and suggest how I can integrate them into my panel discussion about protecting small businesses."

3. **Framing Opinions with Data:**

   - "Gather statistics and recent findings that support my opinion on [topic]. Frame these talking points in a way that seamlessly incorporates my personal insights for a speech or panel."

   - *Example*: "Find key data on remote work productivity and show how I can use it to support my experience in managing remote teams during a keynote speech."

Initial Client Communications

1. **Introducing Yourself and Services:**

   - "Compose an introductory email to a new client that reflects my experience in [your field] and highlights how my services align with their needs. Keep the tone [e.g., friendly, professional, reassuring]."

- *Example*: "Write an introductory email for a potential client looking for consulting services in digital marketing. Emphasize my track record with successful campaigns and my approach to strategic growth."

2. **Highlighting Solutions:**

- "Draft an email that introduces a tailored solution for [specific client need], using details from our past conversation to show understanding and relevance. Keep the message concise and value-driven."

- *Example*: "Create an email for a client interested in boosting their social media engagement, referencing our recent call and proposing a customized content strategy."

3. **Setting Up Initial Meetings:**

- "Write a professional email inviting a client to a discovery meeting. Include a brief overview of what we'll discuss, referencing their expressed interests or challenges from prior communication."

- *Example*: "Draft a meeting invitation for a client interested in scaling their e-commerce business, mentioning that we will explore potential SEO and PPC strategies based on their current goals."

Follow-Up Client Communications

1. **Post-Meeting Follow-Up:**
    *   "Write a follow-up email summarizing our recent meeting with [client's name] and outline the next steps. Mention key points discussed to show attentiveness and alignment."
    *   *Example*: "Create a follow-up email for a client after a strategy session about their website redesign, including a summary of the proposed design changes and timeline."

2. **Checking In for Feedback:**
    *   "Draft a check-in email to a client asking for feedback on [project/service]. Ensure the tone is open and encouraging, inviting honest input and offering continued support."
    *   *Example*: "Write an email to follow up with a client after the implementation of a new CRM system, asking for their feedback on its impact so far and offering further assistance."

3. **Reminding Clients of Upcoming Deadlines:**
    *   "Compose a reminder email for a client

about an upcoming deadline or milestone. Reference prior conversations to keep the tone collaborative and supportive."

- *Example*: "Draft a friendly reminder email for a client regarding the upcoming deadline for their product launch, mentioning any outstanding tasks that need their input."

Personalized Client Responses

1. **Addressing Client Concerns:**

   - "Write a response email that addresses [specific client concern]. Reference past conversations to show understanding and offer a clear solution."

   - *Example*: "Compose an email addressing a client's concern about the timeline for their marketing campaign, reiterating our prior discussion and proposing adjustments to meet their needs."

2. **Providing Detailed Updates:**

   - "Draft an email update for [client's name] on the progress of [specific project]. Include recent developments, next steps, and any changes since our last communication."

- *Example*: "Write an update for a client on the progress of their brand refresh project, detailing completed stages and what's planned next."

3. **Personalized Recommendations:**

   - "Create an email with tailored recommendations for [client's name], based on prior feedback and current objectives. Ensure the message shows your understanding of their business and aligns with their goals."

   - *Example*: "Draft an email for a client who wants to expand their customer base, recommending specific outreach and content strategies that align with their budget and market."

Follow-Ups After Deliverables

1. **Confirming Satisfaction and Next Steps:**

   - "Compose an email to follow up after delivering [project/deliverable], confirming the client's satisfaction and suggesting the next steps. Reference key points from the last conversation for a personalized touch."

- *Example*: "Create a follow-up email for a client after delivering their website redesign, ensuring they're satisfied and outlining the next steps for launch support."

2. **Offering Continued Support:**

- "Draft an email that offers continued support after completing [service or project]. Mention any potential future services that align with their current goals."

- *Example*: "Write a follow-up email to a client after completing their social media campaign, mentioning additional content optimization services that could further boost engagement."

3. **Thanking Clients for Their Business:**

- "Create a thank-you email for [client's name] to show appreciation for their trust in my services and highlight key achievements of the completed project. Keep the tone warm and professional."

- *Example*: "Draft a thank-you email for a client after completing their quarterly marketing strategy, recapping the main achievements and expressing gratitude for their partnership."

Building Long-Term Client Relationships

1. **Providing Value Beyond Services:**

    *   "Compose an email with useful insights or resources related to [client's industry]. Show that you're invested in their long-term success by offering value beyond the scope of your services."

    *   *Example*: "Write an email to a client in the real estate industry sharing a recent market trend report and a brief analysis of how it could impact their business."

2. **Checking In Periodically:**

    *   "Draft a friendly check-in email for [client's name], mentioning past projects and asking if there's anything new you can assist with. Keep the tone casual and open."

    *   *Example*: "Create a check-in email for a past client in the tech industry, referencing their last app launch and offering help with any new developments."

3. **Announcing New Services or Updates:**

- "Write an email to inform [client's name] about new services or updates that could benefit their business. Reference relevant past conversations to personalize the message."

- *Example*: "Draft an email for a client announcing your new SEO service package, highlighting how it complements the social media strategy you previously worked on together."

Business Decision Support

1. **Analyzing Past Experiences:**

- "Review my past business projects and identify key lessons that can inform my decision on [specific upcoming project or initiative]. Summarize these lessons and how they relate to my current challenge."

- *Example*: "Analyze my previous marketing campaigns and highlight what strategies were most successful to guide my decision on launching a new campaign for a tech product."

2. **Comparative Analysis for Strategic Choices:**

- "Create a pros and cons list for choosing between [Option A] and [Option B], using insights from similar decisions I have made in the past. Include potential risks and opportunities for each."

- *Example*: "Compare the benefits and drawbacks of expanding my business into digital products versus physical goods, referencing past projects where I made similar choices."

3. **Data-Driven Decision Support:**

- "Generate an analysis of key performance metrics from past projects to support my decision on [new business strategy]. Ensure the data is framed to show trends, successes, and areas for caution."

- *Example*: "Review sales data from my last three product launches and identify patterns that could inform the strategy for my next launch."

Personal Project Decisions

1. **Leveraging Personal Insights:**
   - "Reflect on my personal projects from the past five years and summarize what approaches worked best for achieving my goals. Use these insights to guide my decision on starting [new project]."
   - *Example*: "Analyze my previous writing projects to determine what habits and workflows were most effective, to help plan my next book."

2. **Evaluating New Opportunities:**
   - "Create a framework for evaluating whether [new opportunity] aligns with my personal values and long-term goals, based on previous decisions and their outcomes."
   - *Example*: "Develop a decision-making framework to assess if accepting a new consulting role fits with my career path, using past experiences for reference."

3. **Identifying Key Success Factors:**
   - "List the key factors that contributed to my most successful personal projects and

explain how I can apply these factors to [upcoming project]."

- *Example*: "Identify the main elements that led to my successful podcast launch and suggest how I can apply them to starting a video series."

Strategic Planning

1. **Long-Term Strategy Development:**
   - "Draft a strategic plan outline for [specific goal or business objective], drawing from lessons learned during past experiences. Highlight which strategies led to sustainable growth and which to avoid."
   - *Example*: "Create a strategic plan for scaling my freelance writing business based on my past experiences with client acquisition and content production."

2. **Assessing Team and Resource Allocation:**
   - "Analyze how I allocated resources and managed teams in previous projects to help decide the best approach for [new project]. Include insights on what worked well and

what challenges arose."

- *Example*: "Review my past experiences leading marketing teams and suggest the most effective way to structure my current team for an upcoming product launch."

3. **Decision Path Mapping:**

- "Outline potential decision paths for [specific business problem], incorporating past scenarios where I faced similar challenges. Highlight the outcomes of those choices to inform my current decision."

- *Example*: "Map out decision paths for expanding into a new market, referencing past experiences where I scaled operations and the lessons learned."

Risk Management

1. **Identifying Potential Risks:**

- "List potential risks associated with [business decision or project], referencing similar past projects where I encountered challenges. Suggest mitigation strategies based on past outcomes."

- *Example*: "Identify risks for launching a subscription-based service, using my previous experience with SaaS product launches as a guide."

2. **Learning from Mistakes:**
   - "Summarize mistakes from my past projects that could inform better decision-making for [upcoming project]. Include what I learned from each experience and how I can avoid repeating them."
   - *Example*: "Review my past content creation projects and point out any common pitfalls that should be avoided when planning my new blog series."

3. **Scenario Planning:**
   - "Develop a set of 'what if' scenarios for [specific decision], incorporating insights from past projects to predict possible outcomes and guide contingency planning."
   - *Example*: "Create scenarios for launching a crowdfunding campaign for my new product, drawing on lessons learned from my previous fundraising efforts."

Personal Growth and Career Decisions

1. **Aligning with Personal Values:**

   - "Evaluate how my past career decisions aligned with my core values and long-term aspirations. Use these insights to guide whether I should pursue [new career move or project]."

   - *Example*: "Review past job changes and how they aligned with my goals, and use that to decide if this new role fits my career trajectory."

2. **Balancing Priorities:**

   - "Analyze my past methods for balancing personal and professional priorities during major projects. Recommend strategies for maintaining balance while pursuing [specific project]."

   - *Example*: "Review how I managed work-life balance during my last entrepreneurial venture and suggest ways to apply those lessons as I start my new business."

3. **Skill Development Focus:**

- "Identify which skills I developed during past projects were most beneficial to my growth and recommend which skills to focus on for [upcoming project or career goal]."

- *Example*: "Determine which skills gained from previous leadership roles were most valuable and suggest areas to develop for my upcoming team management role."

Career Guidance

1. **Sharing Relevant Experiences:**

- "Draft an email or conversation outline sharing a relevant experience from my career that aligns with [mentee's current challenge]. Include key lessons learned and how these can be applied to their situation."

- *Example*: "Write an email to a mentee struggling with work-life balance, sharing my experience of navigating similar challenges during my early career and the strategies I found effective."

2. **Guiding Through Transitions:**

- "Create personalized advice for a mentee transitioning to [new role or career phase]. Reference my past experiences with similar transitions and the insights I gained."

- *Example*: "Draft advice for a mentee moving from a technical role to a managerial position, including how I handled the shift from individual contributions to team leadership."

3. **Navigating Setbacks:**

- "Compose a message offering encouragement and actionable advice for a mentee facing [specific setback]. Use examples from times I overcame similar obstacles to make the guidance relatable."

- *Example*: "Prepare a message for a mentee who recently had a project fail, sharing how I managed setbacks and bounced back stronger in my own career."

Skill Development

1. **Recommending Skill-Building Paths:**

   - "Draft a personalized learning plan for a mentee who wants to develop [specific skill]. Use examples of how I developed that skill and suggest practical steps or resources."

   - *Example*: "Create a skill-building plan for a mentee looking to improve their public speaking, incorporating the methods I used to build my confidence and effectiveness."

2. **Providing Tips for Continuous Learning:**

   - "Write an advice piece on how to maintain continuous learning in [field/industry]. Share lessons from my own journey of staying updated and relevant in the industry."

   - *Example*: "Draft a guide for a mentee on how to keep learning in digital marketing, highlighting key resources and practices I've relied on."

3. **Guidance for Building Expertise:**

   - "Compose a step-by-step approach for a mentee to build their expertise in [specific area], incorporating strategies I used that were particularly successful."

- *Example*: "Prepare guidance for a mentee aiming to become an expert in project management, including how I gained certification, practical experience, and peer learning."

Leadership and Management Advice

1. **Advice on Leading Teams:**

   - "Create personalized leadership advice for a mentee taking on their first management role. Draw from my experiences leading teams, including challenges I faced and solutions that worked."

   - *Example*: "Draft leadership advice for a mentee who is nervous about their new managerial position, emphasizing team motivation strategies and conflict resolution techniques."

2. **Strategies for Effective Communication:**

   - "Write guidance for a mentee looking to improve communication within their team. Share examples of communication challenges I've navigated and the practices that led to better outcomes."

- *Example*: "Prepare a conversation outline for a mentee struggling with team alignment, offering tips based on my experience with fostering open and effective communication."

3. **Handling Difficult Situations:**

- "Develop an advice piece for a mentee facing a challenging work situation (e.g., dealing with difficult stakeholders). Use examples from times I managed similar situations and offer practical advice."

- *Example*: "Compose advice for a mentee managing a project with tight deadlines and demanding clients, sharing how I handled similar pressure and delivered results."

Personal Development

1. **Encouraging Self-Reflection:**

- "Draft a message encouraging a mentee to engage in self-reflection, sharing how this practice has helped me grow personally and professionally. Include tips for effective self-reflection."

- *Example*: "Create an email for a mentee about the value of journaling and setting aside time for introspection, sharing how this practice influenced my decision-making."

2. **Balancing Work and Life:**

- "Compose tailored advice for a mentee struggling with work-life balance. Share strategies I've implemented to manage my time and priorities effectively."

- *Example*: "Prepare guidance for a mentee who is overworked, providing tips on setting boundaries and finding time for personal interests, based on my experiences."

3. **Building Confidence and Overcoming Impostor Syndrome:**

- "Write an advice piece for a mentee who is dealing with impostor syndrome, sharing stories of when I felt similarly and the steps I took to build confidence."

- *Example*: "Compose an encouraging message for a mentee questioning their skills, including how I overcame self-doubt early in my career."

Long-Term Mentorship Planning

1. **Setting and Reviewing Goals:**
   - "Create a mentorship plan for a mentee that includes setting achievable short-term and long-term goals, drawing from the goal-setting frameworks I've found most effective."
   - *Example*: "Prepare a step-by-step guide for a mentee to set and track career goals over the next year, incorporating milestone checks and motivational tips."

2. **Offering Check-In Advice:**
   - "Draft an email for a quarterly check-in with a mentee, summarizing their progress based on previous discussions and suggesting next steps for continued growth."
   - *Example*: "Write a check-in message for a mentee who has been working on improving their leadership skills, celebrating their wins and identifying areas for further development."

3. **Providing Ongoing Support:**

- "Compose a message for a mentee expressing continued support and offering guidance on new challenges they may face, drawing on my experience in similar situations."

- *Example*: "Create an email for a mentee who recently received a promotion, offering advice on transitioning smoothly and staying confident in their new role."

Coaching on Leadership Development

1. **Sharing Leadership Lessons:**

- "Draft a coaching session outline that shares key lessons from my leadership journey, focusing on [specific leadership trait, e.g., resilience or communication]. Include stories that illustrate these lessons and practical takeaways for the team."

- *Example*: "Create a coaching outline on the importance of resilience, incorporating my experience of leading a team through a major project setback and how we overcame it."

2. **Advising on Leadership Styles:**

   - "Compose advice on how to identify and develop a personal leadership style. Use examples from my own experiences with different leadership approaches and their effectiveness in various contexts."

   - *Example*: "Prepare a guide for a team member on finding their leadership style, sharing how I adapted between directive and collaborative leadership based on team needs."

3. **Addressing Leadership Challenges:**

   - "Develop a coaching session script that helps team members navigate common leadership challenges, such as managing conflict or inspiring a demotivated team. Share strategies I used successfully in similar situations."

   - *Example*: "Write a coaching session script on handling team conflicts, including my experience mediating between two team members with differing perspectives."

Strategic Decision-Making Coaching

1. **Teaching Decision Frameworks:**
   - "Create a leadership coaching guide on decision-making frameworks that I have found effective. Include real-world examples where I applied these frameworks and the outcomes."
   - *Example*: "Develop a coaching guide on using the 'pros and cons' and 'risk-benefit' frameworks, illustrated by my strategic decisions during product development phases."

2. **Advising on Complex Decisions:**
   - "Draft a session where I coach a team member through a complex decision they're facing. Include a step-by-step method I have used to analyze complex problems and make informed choices."
   - *Example*: "Prepare a coaching conversation where I help a team member decide between pursuing two high-priority projects, using my experience in prioritizing and resource management."

3. **Reflecting on Past Decisions:**

    *   "Write a coaching prompt that helps team members learn from past decisions, using my experiences to illustrate how analyzing past outcomes can inform future strategies."

    *   *Example*: "Create a reflective session discussing my experience with a failed project and what lessons I took away to improve future decision-making."

Team Motivation and Engagement

1. **Encouraging a Growth Mindset:**

    *   "Develop a motivational coaching session that emphasizes the importance of a growth mindset. Use stories from my career where embracing challenges led to significant growth for me or my team."

    *   *Example*: "Draft a coaching session on how I turned setbacks into learning opportunities, inspiring team members to see challenges as pathways to development."

2. **Boosting Team Morale:**

   - "Compose a coaching session outline on strategies to boost team morale during tough times. Include examples of techniques I used to maintain positivity and engagement in past projects."

   - *Example*: "Create a coaching guide on leading a team through high-stress periods, sharing how I kept my team motivated and cohesive during a demanding project."

3. **Building Trust and Open Communication:**

   - "Write a coaching conversation that guides team members on fostering trust and open communication within their teams, sharing how I cultivated these elements in my leadership roles."

   - *Example*: "Develop a session outline explaining how I built a culture of transparency and trust by implementing regular check-ins and open feedback loops."

Coaching on Innovation and Creativity

1. **Fostering Creative Thinking:**
   - "Create a coaching plan that encourages team members to think creatively and propose innovative ideas. Share stories of how I successfully led brainstorming sessions and nurtured innovation."
   - *Example*: "Prepare a coaching guide on running effective brainstorming sessions, detailing how I inspired out-of-the-box thinking in my team."

2. **Guiding Through the Innovation Process:**
   - "Compose a session outline on how to manage and implement innovative ideas, using examples of projects where I led innovation and overcame obstacles."
   - *Example*: "Draft a coaching session about managing the innovation process, including my experience developing a new product feature from concept to launch."

3. **Balancing Risk and Creativity:**

- "Develop a coaching session focused on balancing risk with creative ambition. Include examples of when I took calculated risks that paid off and when I adjusted creative ideas to mitigate potential downsides."

- *Example*: "Create a coaching outline for mentoring team members on pursuing bold ideas while assessing potential risks, drawing from my experience launching a high-risk marketing campaign."

Real-Time Leadership Guidance

1. **On-the-Spot Problem Solving:**

- "Draft a playbook for providing real-time guidance when team members face unexpected challenges. Use examples from times when I had to think on my feet and guide the team effectively."

- *Example*: "Create an outline for guiding team members through sudden changes in project scope, drawing from my experience managing last-minute client requests."

2. **Providing Quick Insights During Meetings:**

- "Prepare talking points for offering strategic advice during team meetings where immediate decisions are needed. Include examples of moments I stepped in to provide clarity and direction."

- *Example*: "Draft key points on how to lead a team meeting when decisions on budget reallocation need to be made quickly, referencing how I handled similar scenarios."

3. **Guiding New Leaders in Real Time:**

- "Write coaching prompts for mentoring new leaders during their first leadership challenges. Use stories of my early leadership experiences to provide context and actionable advice."

- *Example*: "Prepare real-time coaching tips for a new team leader handling their first performance review, sharing how I approached my initial reviews and feedback sessions."

Writing Thought Leadership Articles

1. **Identifying Key Industry Trends:**
   - "Draft an outline for a thought leadership article on [specific industry trend], using my experiences and insights to highlight its implications and future direction. Include examples from past projects or observations."
   - *Example*: "Create an article outline discussing the future of remote work, drawing from my experience managing hybrid teams and analyzing current trends."

2. **Providing Unique Perspectives:**
   - "Compose a guest article that presents my unique perspective on [industry topic], incorporating case studies or stories from my career that reinforce my point of view."
   - *Example*: "Draft a guest article on how small businesses can leverage AI technology for growth, using my firsthand experience consulting for startups."

3. **Sharing Lessons Learned:**

- "Write a piece that shares the top lessons I've learned about [industry topic] over my career, and explain how these lessons can benefit others in the field."

- *Example*: "Prepare an article outlining key lessons from my decade of experience in digital marketing and how new marketers can apply these lessons to their strategies."

Contributing to Industry Discussions

1. **Responding to Current Industry Challenges:**

- "Prepare talking points for a LinkedIn post or discussion that addresses [current industry challenge], including my strategic insights and recommendations for moving forward."

- *Example*: "Write talking points for a LinkedIn post about the challenges of adapting to new privacy regulations in digital advertising, incorporating my expertise in compliance and marketing."

2. **Engaging in Q&A Forums:**

- "Create responses to common questions in [industry-related forum or online group], showcasing my expertise and providing actionable advice or thought-provoking insights."

- *Example*: "Draft replies for a Q&A session on a tech industry forum discussing effective project management tools and techniques."

3. **Adding Value to Ongoing Conversations:**

- "Draft a thought leadership comment for an ongoing industry conversation on [specific topic], sharing my perspective based on past experiences and professional insights."

- *Example*: "Compose a comment for a discussion on the impact of emerging AI technologies in healthcare, referencing my experience in tech strategy consulting."

Preparing for Podcasts

1. **Developing Key Talking Points:**

- "Create a list of key talking points for my upcoming podcast appearance on [topic], incorporating my personal insights and experiences that highlight my expertise."

- *Example*: "Prepare talking points for a podcast on the evolution of content marketing, including stories about how I adapted strategies over time."

2. **Summarizing Personal Stories:**

- "Outline two or three impactful stories from my career that align with the theme of [podcast topic]. Summarize each with a clear beginning, middle, and end, and include the lessons learned."

- *Example*: "Summarize stories from my career that illustrate innovative problem-solving in product development for a podcast on creative leadership."

3. **Framing Thought-Provoking Questions:**

- "Draft a few questions I could propose or discuss on a podcast to stimulate deep conversation on [specific industry topic]. Ensure the questions align with my thought leadership voice."

- *Example*: "Create questions for a podcast on sustainable business practices that encourage discussion about long-term benefits versus short-term costs."

Writing Guest Articles

1. **Presenting Original Research or Insights:**

   - "Draft a guest article proposal that shares findings from my research or analysis on [industry topic]. Highlight key takeaways and why they matter to [target audience]."

   - *Example*: "Write a guest article on the insights I've gained from analyzing marketing trends over the past year and how businesses can leverage this data."

2. **Making Predictions:**

   - "Compose an article that outlines my predictions for [industry or topic] in the next 5-10 years, using data, experiences, and emerging trends to back up my forecasts."

   - *Example*: "Create an article predicting how e-commerce will evolve in the next decade, based on my consulting experiences and recent technological advancements."

3. **Offering Practical Advice:**

   - "Write a guest article that provides practical advice for professionals in [field], incorporating examples and actionable tips drawn from my own practices."

- *Example*: "Prepare an article on effective strategies for personal branding in the tech industry, including tips from my own journey as a thought leader."

Enhancing Industry Reputation

1. **Building Thought Leadership on Social Media:**
   - "Compose a series of social media posts that reflect my thought leadership in [industry], using a mix of personal insights, data points, and trending topics to engage my audience."
   - *Example*: "Write a series of posts for LinkedIn showcasing my top takeaways from recent industry conferences and how they apply to emerging professionals."

2. **Publishing White Papers or Reports:**
   - "Create an outline for a white paper on [topic], synthesizing my expertise and past project data to present an authoritative analysis that positions me as a thought leader."

- *Example*: "Draft an outline for a white paper on the impacts of automation in logistics, combining my research and consulting experience."

3. **Speaking at Conferences or Panels:**

   - "Develop a list of talking points for a conference presentation on [industry topic], incorporating my key experiences and unique perspectives."

   - *Example*: "Prepare talking points for a conference presentation on leading digital transformation initiatives, supported by stories from projects I've overseen."

Ongoing Thought Leadership

1. **Regular Industry Updates:**

   - "Draft content for a recurring newsletter or blog series that provides updates and my analysis on [industry developments]. Include reflections from my professional experience."

- *Example*: "Create content for a monthly newsletter focused on the latest trends in tech innovation and my commentary on their potential impacts."

2. **Providing a Unique Spin on Common Topics:**

- "Write an article or post that offers an unconventional take on [commonly discussed industry topic], backed by examples from my career that highlight why my perspective is different."

- *Example*: "Draft a post for a business blog offering a new perspective on agile methodology, incorporating stories from when I adapted agile principles in unexpected ways."

3. **Sharing 'Behind-the-Scenes' Insights:**

- "Compose a piece that shares behind-the-scenes insights from [specific project or experience], offering lessons and strategies that aren't commonly discussed."

- *Example*: "Write a behind-the-scenes article on leading a major company rebranding effort, including challenges faced and lessons learned."

Client Interactions

1. **Personalized Client Outreach:**

   - "Draft a personalized email introducing myself and my services to [client's name]. Make sure it reflects my [e.g., warm, professional, enthusiastic] tone and includes a reference to their specific needs based on our previous conversations."

   - *Example*: "Create an introductory email for a potential client who needs marketing strategy consulting. Highlight my experience and how it aligns with their recent expansion plans."

2. **Project Updates:**

   - "Compose an email providing [client's name] with an update on the current status of [specific project]. Include highlights of recent progress, next steps, and a brief overview of any issues resolved, using a [e.g., professional, transparent, collaborative] tone."

   - *Example*: "Draft a project status update for a client on their app development project, mentioning recent milestones and the timeline for the next phase."

3. **Client Check-Ins:**

- "Write a check-in email for [client's name] to ask how they are finding [product/service] so far and if they have any feedback or questions. Keep the tone friendly and open to encourage engagement."

- *Example*: "Prepare a check-in email for a client after the first month of using my financial consulting services, asking for feedback and offering a brief follow-up call."

Networking Follow-Ups

1. **Thank You Emails:**

- "Draft a thank-you email for [contact's name] after our recent meeting or event. Include a specific mention of what I appreciated about our conversation and express my interest in staying in touch."

- *Example*: "Write a thank-you email for a professional I met at a tech conference, highlighting a shared interest in AI advancements and suggesting a follow-up chat."

2. **Post-Event Follow-Ups:**

- "Create a follow-up email for [contact's name] after attending [specific event or webinar]. Mention key takeaways from the event and propose a future discussion or collaboration."

- *Example*: "Compose a follow-up email for a colleague I met at a marketing seminar, discussing insights from a presentation on content strategy and suggesting we share ideas over coffee."

3. **Reconnecting with Contacts:**

- "Write an email to reconnect with [old contact's name], referencing our last conversation and updating them on my recent work or achievements. Keep it friendly and genuine."

- *Example*: "Draft an email to reconnect with a former client, mentioning our past collaboration on a project and sharing news about a recent related success."

Automated Responses

1. **Out-of-Office Replies:**

   - "Compose an automated out-of-office email that reflects my [e.g., friendly, professional] tone. Include an expected return date and alternative contacts for urgent matters."

   - *Example*: "Create an out-of-office reply stating that I'm unavailable for the week due to a conference, and direct urgent inquiries to my assistant."

2. **Confirmation Emails:**

   - "Write an automated email confirming [appointment, booking, or meeting] with [client's name]. Ensure the tone is polite and includes any necessary details or attachments."

   - *Example*: "Prepare a confirmation email for a client confirming our scheduled consultation, including the date, time, and video call link."

3. **Thank You for Your Inquiry:**

   - "Draft an automated response thanking [client or contact] for their inquiry about [specific service or topic]. Indicate when they can expect a more detailed reply."

- *Example*: "Write a thank-you email that acknowledges a new client's interest in my design services and mentions that I'll follow up with more information within 24 hours."

Sales and Follow-Up Emails

1. **Personalized Sales Outreach:**
   - "Draft a sales email introducing [product/service] to [client or group], tailored to their specific needs and challenges as discussed in previous interactions. Keep the tone personable and informative."
   - *Example*: "Compose a sales email for a potential client outlining the benefits of my SEO consulting services, referencing our recent conversation about their website traffic goals."

2. **Follow-Up After a Proposal:**
   - "Write a follow-up email to [client's name] after submitting a proposal for [project]. Ensure the tone is proactive and offers to answer any questions they might have."

- *Example*: "Draft an email following up on a marketing proposal submitted to a potential client, reminding them of key points and inviting them to schedule a discussion."

3. **Re-Engagement Emails:**

- "Compose an email to re-engage a past client who hasn't interacted with my services in a while. Include an update on new offerings or recent successes to spark interest."

- *Example*: "Write a re-engagement email to a former client, highlighting a new service I launched that aligns with their past projects."

Personalized Email Campaigns

1. **Educational Email Series:**

- "Create the first email of an educational series on [topic], tailored to [audience] and written in my [e.g., informative, engaging, inspiring] voice. Ensure it provides value and invites interaction."

- *Example*: "Draft the first email in a series on productivity tips for entrepreneurs, sharing a key strategy I've used successfully."

2. **Client Onboarding Emails:**

   - "Compose an onboarding email for new clients using [product/service]. Outline the first steps they should take, and offer assistance to make their experience smooth and welcoming."

   - *Example*: "Write an onboarding email for new clients of my consulting service, explaining how to schedule their first session and access initial resources."

3. **Survey or Feedback Requests:**

   - "Draft an email requesting feedback from [client's name] after [project/service completion]. Ensure the tone is appreciative and emphasizes that their input is valued."

   - *Example*: "Create a feedback request email for a client who recently completed a training session, asking them to share their thoughts on the experience."

Scheduling Appointments

1. **Setting Up Meetings:**
   - "Compose an email to schedule a meeting with [contact's name], considering my availability on [dates/times]. Ensure the message is polite and provides alternative time slots for flexibility."
   - *Example*: "Draft an email to schedule a client check-in meeting next week, suggesting times on Tuesday and Thursday afternoons."

2. **Confirming Appointments:**
   - "Create an email template for confirming scheduled meetings with [clients/contacts]. Include the date, time, and location, and offer any necessary preparatory details."
   - *Example*: "Prepare a confirmation email for a video call with a new client, detailing the meeting link and agenda."

3. **Rescheduling Appointments:**
   - "Write a polite and professional email template for rescheduling appointments, explaining the need for the change and offering new available time slots."

- *Example*: "Compose an email for rescheduling a project status meeting due to an unexpected conflict, providing options for later in the week."

Managing Your Calendar

1. **Daily Schedule Overview:**
   - "Generate a daily email that summarizes my schedule, highlighting key appointments and important tasks for the day. Ensure it reflects my working habit of prioritizing morning productivity."
   - *Example*: "Prepare a morning summary that shows today's meetings, top tasks, and dedicated focus time blocks."

2. **Weekly Planning:**
   - "Draft a weekly overview that outlines major meetings, deadlines, and personal appointments for the upcoming week. Organize it in a way that supports my preference for front-loading the week with major tasks."

- *Example*: "Create a weekly plan email that summarizes client calls on Monday and Wednesday and time set aside for strategic work on Thursday."

3. **Time Blocking for Productivity:**

   - "Plan my calendar for [day/week], blocking time for focused work sessions, breaks, and meetings in line with my typical work habits. Prioritize tasks that require deep focus in the morning."

   - *Example*: "Block time on Wednesday for deep work in the morning and shorter task sessions in the afternoon, leaving a slot open for last-minute meetings."

Task Prioritization

1. **Prioritizing Daily Tasks:**

   - "List and prioritize my tasks for the day based on importance and deadlines. Use my working habit of tackling complex tasks early and leaving simpler ones for the end of the day."

- *Example*: "Create today's task list, putting the high-priority project draft at the top, followed by emails, and ending with administrative work."

2. **Managing High-Priority Deadlines:**

   - "Compose a task schedule that highlights high-priority items with upcoming deadlines. Organize the tasks in a way that reflects my habit of working in 90-minute focus blocks."

   - *Example*: "Develop a prioritized task list for the week with the top project tasks grouped into 90-minute sessions, with review periods on Friday."

3. **Balancing Long-Term and Short-Term Tasks:**

   - "Prepare a plan that helps balance long-term project goals with short-term daily tasks. Align it with my working habit of dedicating certain afternoons for strategic planning."

   - *Example*: "Draft a task plan that includes time for ongoing project research on Tuesday afternoon and daily administrative tasks in the last 30 minutes of each day."

Task Delegation and Follow-Ups

1. **Delegating Tasks to Team Members:**

    *   "Draft an email delegating [specific task] to [team member's name]. Include clear instructions, deadlines, and resources they might need. Keep the tone supportive and informative."

    *   *Example*: "Write an email assigning the task of preparing a presentation to my assistant, detailing the main points to cover and the due date."

2. **Task Follow-Up Reminders:**

    *   "Generate follow-up reminders for tasks I've delegated, ensuring the tone is polite and reflects my collaborative working style. Schedule these for [specific days]."

    *   *Example*: "Compose follow-up reminders for a report I assigned, set to go out one day before the deadline to check in on progress."

3. **Tracking Task Progress:**

    - "Create a template for tracking the progress of key tasks and projects in my calendar. Include automatic reminders that align with my habit of reviewing progress mid-week."

    - *Example*: "Add a calendar reminder to check on project status updates every Wednesday afternoon and Friday morning."

Scheduling Personal Appointments

1. **Adding Personal Commitments:**

    - "Add personal appointments, such as [doctor's appointment or family events], to my calendar and balance them with work tasks so that they don't disrupt my peak productivity periods."

    - *Example*: "Schedule a doctor's appointment on Thursday morning and adjust the work calendar to keep the afternoon open for focus time."

2. **Scheduling Breaks for Work-Life Balance:**

   - "Plan my day to include breaks at times when I typically feel less productive, ensuring these breaks help maintain work-life balance."

   - *Example*: "Block off 15-minute breaks in my calendar at 10:30 a.m. and 3:00 p.m. to maintain energy and focus."

3. **Coordinating Work and Personal Priorities:**

   - "Create a balanced schedule that aligns work deadlines with personal priorities, reflecting my practice of setting boundaries for after-work hours."

   - *Example*: "Schedule work tasks to end by 6:00 p.m. and add a reminder to turn off work notifications at that time."

Real-Time Adjustments

1. **Adapting to Last-Minute Changes:**

   - "Compose a quick adjustment plan for my calendar in response to [unexpected meeting or priority change]. Shift lower-priority tasks as needed."

- *Example*: "Reschedule an afternoon task to accommodate a last-minute client meeting, keeping the top-priority tasks in the morning intact."

2. **Urgent Task Insertion:**

   - "Add an urgent task to my day's schedule and shift other tasks to make room. Ensure my key work habits, such as maintaining a midday break, are still respected."

   - *Example*: "Insert an urgent task related to a client report due tomorrow and move today's admin work to the end of the day."

3. **Communicating Schedule Changes:**

   - "Draft a quick email notifying relevant parties of a change in my schedule due to [reason]. Keep the tone professional and informative."

   - *Example*: "Write an email informing the project team that today's meeting has been moved to Friday due to an urgent client call."

Crafting Social Media Posts

1. **Sharing Industry Insights:**

   - "Draft a LinkedIn post that shares my latest thoughts on [industry trend or news]. Ensure the tone reflects my [e.g., expert, conversational, enthusiastic] voice and invites engagement from professionals in [industry]."

   - *Example*: "Create a LinkedIn post discussing recent advancements in AI and their implications for small businesses. Highlight key takeaways and add a question at the end to encourage discussion."

2. **Announcing Achievements or Milestones:**

   - "Compose a Twitter thread that celebrates [specific personal or business milestone], keeping the tone authentic and motivational. Include reflections on the journey and express gratitude."

   - *Example*: "Write a Twitter thread celebrating the completion of my 100th project as a freelance graphic designer, sharing key lessons learned and tips for fellow designers."

3. **Educational Content:**

- "Generate an Instagram carousel post that breaks down [specific concept or topic] in an easy-to-understand way, reflecting my teaching style. Ensure the tone stays informative and approachable."

- *Example*: "Create an Instagram carousel post explaining the basics of SEO for beginners, using simple visuals and step-by-step tips."

Sharing Personal Stories

1. **Posting Success Stories:**

- "Draft a LinkedIn post sharing a personal story of overcoming a challenge related to [your work or project]. Keep the tone inspiring and include key lessons learned."

- *Example*: "Write a post about the time I launched my first product and faced unexpected hurdles, focusing on how I adapted and what I learned from the experience."

2. **Behind-the-Scenes Content:**

   - "Compose an Instagram post that shares behind-the-scenes insights from [recent project or event]. Use a conversational tone and include anecdotes that reflect my authentic self."

   - *Example*: "Create an Instagram post with a behind-the-scenes look at preparing for my keynote speech, sharing snapshots of my workspace and notes."

3. **Reflective Posts:**

   - "Write a Twitter post reflecting on [personal or professional growth moment]. Ensure the tone is thoughtful and adds value to my followers' feed."

   - *Example*: "Draft a tweet reflecting on my career journey from starting as an intern to leading my own team, sharing the biggest takeaway that shaped my path."

Scheduling Social Media Content

1. **Weekly Content Plan:**

   - "Create a weekly schedule of social media posts that includes [e.g., motivational quotes, personal stories, educational content]. Ensure each post stays true to my voice and personal brand."

   - *Example*: "Prepare a weekly social media plan with posts on Monday for motivation, Wednesday for educational tips in marketing, and Friday for a personal story or reflection."

2. **Timed Campaigns:**

   - "Develop a social media content plan for a [specific campaign or launch], spacing out posts over a period of [timeframe]. Ensure the content builds anticipation and reflects my brand tone."

   - *Example*: "Plan a series of posts leading up to the launch of my new book, starting with teasers and ending with a launch-day video."

3. **Balancing Content Types:**

- "Create a balanced posting schedule that mixes promotional content with engaging and informative posts. Ensure that each type of post aligns with my brand voice and doesn't feel overly salesy."

- *Example*: "Draft a content plan for the next month that includes two promotional posts per week, balanced with personal insights and industry tips."

Expanding Reach and Engagement

1. **Collaborative Posts:**

- "Write a social media post that tags [colleague/influencer] and shares their recent work or thoughts on [topic]. Ensure the tone is supportive and highlights my connection to them."

- *Example*: "Draft a post tagging a colleague who published a study on remote work, sharing my thoughts on their insights and inviting further discussion."

2. **Cross-Promotion:**

- "Compose a post that promotes my [blog post, podcast episode, or YouTube video] across platforms, adapting the content slightly for each social media channel while maintaining my authentic voice."

- *Example*: "Create a LinkedIn post and a corresponding Instagram story promoting my latest blog on leadership skills, each tailored to fit the platform's style."

3. **Trendy or Timely Posts:**

- "Draft a social media post that taps into [current trend or popular topic] while relating it back to my expertise. Keep the tone timely and reflective of my personal brand."

- *Example*: "Write a Twitter post linking a recent viral trend to key lessons in digital marketing, with a playful yet professional tone."

Automating Social Media Tasks

1. **Creating Post Templates:**

   - "Develop a set of templates for recurring social media posts (e.g., #ThrowbackThursday, weekly tips). Ensure each template maintains my voice and can be quickly adapted with new content."

   - *Example*: "Create a template for weekly LinkedIn tips on productivity, using a format that starts with a question and ends with a call-to-action."

2. **Scheduling Content Reminders:**

   - "Set reminders for me to review or update scheduled posts that align with my planned campaigns, ensuring my content stays relevant and timely."

   - *Example*: "Add a calendar reminder to check scheduled posts for next week's product launch and update any time-sensitive details."

3. **Automating Content Curation:**

- "Write a script or plan for automating the collection of relevant industry news and insights that I can share on my social media. Ensure it pulls articles that reflect my areas of expertise."

- *Example*: "Set up an automated content curation process that gathers the latest articles on digital marketing trends for my weekly Twitter and LinkedIn posts."

Commenting on Industry Peers' Posts

1. **Providing Insightful Feedback:**

- "Write a comment on [peer's name]'s recent post about [topic], sharing my perspective and adding a unique insight from my experience. Ensure the comment feels genuine and aligns with my [e.g., supportive, thoughtful] style."

- *Example*: "Draft a comment for a colleague's LinkedIn post on AI in healthcare, adding my insights from recent projects in tech strategy and emphasizing shared views."

2. **Asking Follow-Up Questions:**

- "Compose a comment that shows genuine interest in [peer's name]'s post by asking a thoughtful follow-up question that encourages further conversation."

- *Example*: "Create a comment for a Twitter post about the challenges of remote work, asking 'What strategies have you found most effective for keeping your team engaged?'"

3. **Sharing Related Resources or Experiences:**

- "Write a comment for [contact's name]'s post where I share a relevant resource or my related experience. Keep the tone collaborative and informative."

- *Example*: "Draft a LinkedIn comment on a post about productivity hacks, sharing an article I wrote on time management or a strategy that worked for me."

Engaging with Followers

1. **Responding to Comments and Continuing Conversations**

   - Prompt: "Generate replies for comments on my recent [type of post] to keep the conversation going and show appreciation. Ensure replies reflect my [e.g., friendly, professional, humorous] tone."

   - *Example*: "Write responses for comments on my LinkedIn post about productivity tips, adding extra insights and thanking followers for their input."

   - Prompt: "Compose supportive comments for followers' posts sharing challenges or achievements in [related field]. Use an empathetic, positive tone to reinforce community and motivation."

   - *Example*: "Write an encouraging comment on a follower's post about overcoming a tough deadline, sharing a motivational insight from my experience."

2. **Starting Conversations and Inviting Participation**

- Prompt: "Write a social media post that asks an open-ended question related to [your field or expertise] to spark conversation among my followers. Ensure it aligns with my personal brand."

- *Example*: "Create a Facebook post asking, 'What's the biggest challenge you face when starting a new project?' and share my perspective in the comments to keep the discussion going."

- Prompt: "Create a LinkedIn poll that invites my network to weigh in on [specific topic or trend], ensuring the tone is engaging and prompts thoughtful participation."

- *Example*: "Create a poll asking followers, 'Which remote work tool has been most beneficial for your productivity?' with options like video conferencing, task management, and communication apps."

3. **Engaging with Followers' Own Posts**

- Prompt: "Draft comments for engaging with followers by responding to their posts about [specific topic]. Keep responses genuine, encouraging, and aligned with my brand voice."

- *Example*: "Comment on a follower's post about their career milestone, congratulating them and asking about their future goals."

Engaging with Clients

1. **Acknowledging Client Success:**
   - "Draft a comment congratulating [client's name] on their recent achievement or post about [specific topic]. Reflect my [e.g., warm, enthusiastic] tone and subtly reinforce my connection to their success."
   - *Example*: "Create a LinkedIn comment for a client's post celebrating a product launch, congratulating them and mentioning how great it was to collaborate."

2. **Responding to Client Questions or Mentions:**
   - "Compose a response to [client's name]'s question or mention on social media, ensuring the reply is informative and reflects my professional yet friendly tone."
   - *Example*: "Draft a response for a client who tagged me in a question about digital marketing trends, providing a concise answer and offering to discuss more."

3. **Building Relationships Through Engagement:**

- "Write comments for client posts that show genuine interest in their content, fostering stronger professional connections."

- *Example*: "Create a LinkedIn comment for a client's update on a new business development, expressing interest and asking how they're planning to approach their next step."

Engaging in Industry Discussions

1. **Adding Value to Trending Topics:**

- "Write a comment on a trending post in [industry group or topic], sharing my perspective and inviting others to contribute. Ensure the comment aligns with my [e.g., insightful, constructive] tone."

- *Example*: "Compose a comment for a LinkedIn discussion on the impact of hybrid work models, sharing my observations and asking the group what challenges they face most."

2. **Disagreeing Constructively:**

   - "Draft a comment that respectfully shares my differing opinion on [specific topic], offering an alternative perspective backed by my experience."

   - *Example*: "Create a comment on a Twitter thread about SEO strategies where I provide a counterpoint and include an example of when my approach led to positive results."

3. **Highlighting Collaborative Ideas:**

   - "Write a comment that builds on someone else's post by suggesting a collaborative idea or expanding on their point. Keep the tone collaborative and positive."

   - *Example*: "Draft a comment for an industry peer's post on marketing automation, suggesting ways this could be integrated with personalized content strategies."

Keeping Engagement Consistent

1. **Daily Engagement Plan:**

   - "Create a daily engagement plan that outlines which posts to comment on and what types of comments to make (e.g., supportive, insightful, questions). Ensure these align with my authentic communication style."

   - *Example*: "Draft a plan for engaging with five key posts per day on LinkedIn, including thought leadership content, peer achievements, and client updates."

2. **Automated Comment Templates:**

   - "Develop a set of templates for common types of comments, such as congratulatory notes, questions, and insight-sharing. Ensure these can be customized easily while reflecting my voice."

   - *Example*: "Create a congratulatory template for career updates, starting with 'Congratulations on your achievement! I'm excited to see what's next for you in [mention field or project].'"

3. **Scheduling Comment Reminders:**

- "Set up reminders to engage with posts at optimal times (e.g., mornings and afternoons), keeping my interaction consistent and visible."

- *Example*: "Create reminders to comment on relevant posts during peak engagement hours to increase visibility and connection."

Special Engagement Occasions

1. **Holiday or Event-Based Comments:**

- "Draft comments for [upcoming holiday or event], where I engage with followers or clients' posts, wishing them well and sharing a relevant note. Keep the tone festive and in line with my brand."

- *Example*: "Create a set of holiday-themed comments for client posts during the end-of-year season, sharing best wishes and reflective thoughts."

2. **Responding to Milestones and Announcements:**

- "Write comments for congratulating industry peers or clients on major announcements (e.g., new roles, business expansions). Make sure each one reflects my enthusiasm and supportive nature."

- *Example*: "Draft a congratulatory comment for a client announcing a merger, mentioning the exciting future ahead and offering my support."

3. **Special Recognition Comments:**

- "Compose comments that recognize followers or clients who contribute valuable insights or consistently engage with my posts. Keep the tone appreciative and warm."

- *Example*: "Create a comment to acknowledge a follower who frequently interacts with my content, thanking them for their thoughtful contributions."

Curating Content for Personal Use

1. **Finding Industry-Specific Articles:**

    •   "Curate a list of the latest articles on [industry topic or trend] that align with my expertise in [field]. Ensure these are from reputable sources and include a brief summary for each."

    •   *Example*: "Find the latest articles on digital marketing trends, including summaries of key insights from reliable sources like HubSpot and MarketingProfs."

2. **Gathering Educational Videos:**

    •   "Compile a list of educational videos on [topic] that match my level of expertise. Include a mix of beginner and advanced content to cover different angles of the subject."

    •   *Example*: "Gather videos explaining AI ethics and applications in tech, suitable for someone with an intermediate understanding of the field."

3. **Recommending Podcasts for Insight:**

- "Suggest podcasts related to [topic] that feature expert discussions, interviews, or case studies. Focus on episodes that align with my interest in [specific industry or niche]."

- *Example*: "Recommend podcasts that cover leadership strategies in business, especially those featuring CEOs or thought leaders sharing their experiences."

Curating Content to Share on Social Media

1. **Finding Shareable News Articles:**

- "Curate current news articles on [industry topic] that are informative and worth sharing with my audience. Include a brief note on why each piece is relevant and impactful."

- *Example*: "Find recent news articles about sustainable business practices that I can share on LinkedIn, with a note on how they connect to current industry efforts."

2. **Sourcing Engaging Videos:**

    - "Compile a set of engaging and informative videos related to [topic] that I can share on my social media. Ensure these videos align with my [e.g., educational, inspiring, analytical] brand tone."

    - *Example*: "Find TED Talks and expert panels on innovative startup strategies that would interest my LinkedIn followers."

3. **Recommending Niche Podcasts for Followers:**

    - "Select podcasts related to [topic] that my audience would find valuable. Include short descriptions of why each episode is worth listening to and its main highlights."

    - *Example*: "Curate a list of marketing podcasts focusing on social media strategy tips, with brief summaries of each episode's key takeaways."

Curating Content for Newsletters

1. **Selecting Newsletter Highlights:**

   - "Curate a list of three key articles, videos, or podcasts for my upcoming newsletter on [topic]. Include why each piece is relevant to my readers and how it ties into my recent discussions."

   - *Example*: "Gather three content pieces for my monthly newsletter on leadership trends, featuring a thought-provoking article, a video panel, and a podcast interview."

2. **Creating a Weekly Reading List:**

   - "Compile a weekly reading list with top articles and studies on [topic]. Summarize each in a few sentences and suggest why my readers should pay attention to them."

   - *Example*: "Create a weekly reading list of the best articles on remote work culture, including summaries and key points that would benefit HR professionals."

3. **Curating 'Top Picks' Content:**

- "Choose a 'Top Picks' selection of articles, videos, and podcasts that align with my expertise in [field]. These will be featured in my newsletter with a brief note on why I recommend each."

- *Example*: "Curate a 'Top Picks' section for my newsletter on project management, with content highlighting new tools and methods used in the industry."

Automated Content Suggestions

1. **Setting Up Content Alerts:**

- "Set up alerts or automated notifications for new articles, podcasts, or videos on [specific topic]. Ensure they are filtered by credibility and relevance to my professional interests."

- *Example*: "Create content alerts for the latest developments in blockchain technology, highlighting only those from reputable tech publications."

2. **Daily Content Digest:**
   - "Prepare a daily content digest with three to five pieces of content related to [topic], including a mix of articles, videos, and podcasts. Ensure a summary and source credibility check for each item."
   - *Example*: "Generate a daily digest of articles, interviews, and expert panels on productivity hacks, with a focus on insights from leaders in the field."

3. **Content Curation with Filters:**
   - "Compile a curated list of content on [topic], filtering for recent publications (e.g., published within the last month) and focusing on expert opinions and research-backed findings."
   - *Example*: "Create a list of recent articles on machine learning, focusing on research publications and expert opinion pieces published in the past month."

Customizing Curated Content

1. **Tailoring Content Summaries:**

    *   "Summarize curated content in a way that reflects my voice and aligns with my brand tone. Include insights on how each piece ties back to my current focus or ongoing projects."

    *   *Example*: "Summarize articles on productivity for my LinkedIn posts, with a reflection on how these ideas align with my recent talks on workplace efficiency."

2. **Adapting Content for Social Media:**

    *   "Create social media posts that share curated articles or videos with an engaging caption that reflects my authentic voice. Include a call-to-action encouraging followers to discuss or share their thoughts."

    *   *Example*: "Draft LinkedIn and Twitter posts summarizing an article on AI in healthcare, with a personal take on its importance and a question to engage my audience."

3. **Curating Theme-Based Content:**

- "Select content related to [specific theme, e.g., innovation, leadership, creativity] that aligns with my upcoming social media campaign. Include a brief explanation of how each piece contributes to the theme."

- *Example*: "Curate content for a week-long series on LinkedIn about innovation in tech, featuring articles, videos, and podcasts that illustrate the theme with clear connections."

Advanced Content Curation

1. **Comparative Content Analysis:**

- "Compile a curated set of articles and videos that present different viewpoints on [topic]. Summarize each perspective and provide a note on how these contrasting views contribute to a deeper understanding."

- *Example*: "Curate content on the pros and cons of remote work, summarizing different viewpoints from company leaders and workforce analysts."

2. **Highlighting Thought Leaders:**

- "Curate content that features prominent thought leaders in [industry or topic], including their articles, interviews, and talks. Add a summary of their key messages and relevance to my audience."

- *Example*: "Select content from leaders in sustainable fashion, summarizing their main points and why their work is significant to industry trends."

3. **Anticipating Emerging Trends:**

- "Find content that discusses emerging trends in [field] and summarize them for a forward-looking post or newsletter. Highlight any early indicators and potential implications."

- *Example*: "Gather content on upcoming trends in digital marketing, summarizing new approaches in AI tools and personalized customer experiences."

Initial Crisis Response

1. **Crafting an Immediate Public Statement:**
   - "Draft an initial public statement addressing [specific issue or crisis]. The tone should be sincere and transparent, acknowledging the issue and outlining immediate next steps."
   - *Example*: "Compose a public statement for a data breach incident, explaining the situation, acknowledging the breach, and reassuring stakeholders of the measures being taken to secure data."

2. **Addressing Stakeholder Concerns:**
   - "Create a message for stakeholders that clearly explains the situation and our response plan for [specific crisis]. Ensure the tone is professional and empathetic, reassuring them of our commitment to resolution."
   - *Example*: "Prepare an email for key stakeholders about a product recall, detailing the problem, steps being taken to resolve it, and expected timelines for updates."

3. **Preparing Talking Points for Interviews:**

   - "Develop talking points for media interviews or press conferences addressing [specific crisis]. Include clear messages that align with our values and provide an honest assessment of the situation."

   - *Example*: "Draft talking points for an interview discussing an environmental incident, focusing on our environmental commitments and corrective actions being taken."

Managing Social Media Reactions

1. **Crafting Social Media Responses:**

   - "Write a set of social media replies addressing comments or concerns related to [crisis topic]. Ensure the responses maintain a compassionate and informative tone."

- *Example*: "Prepare responses for Twitter users asking about delays in customer service due to a sudden issue, showing empathy and explaining what's being done to resolve the problem."

2. **Proactive Social Media Post:**

   - "Create a social media post addressing [crisis topic] proactively to inform and reassure followers. Make sure the message is aligned with our voice and transparent about the next steps."

   - *Example*: "Draft an Instagram and Facebook post addressing service outages, explaining the cause, current progress toward resolution, and an estimated time for full restoration."

3. **Handling Misinformation:**

   - "Write a response to counter misinformation circulating about [specific crisis]. Ensure the tone is factual and calm, correcting inaccuracies while maintaining trust and authority."

   - *Example*: "Compose a LinkedIn post to correct false claims about company layoffs, emphasizing transparency and providing accurate information."

Communicating with Internal Teams

1. **Team Briefing Memo:**

   - "Draft a memo to internal teams outlining the details of [specific crisis], our response plan, and how we're communicating with the public. The tone should be supportive and informative."

   - *Example*: "Create a memo for internal teams explaining the recent security breach, detailing their role in managing the situation, and providing key messages to share if asked."

2. **Employee FAQ for Consistency:**

   - "Prepare an internal FAQ document addressing potential questions employees may have about [crisis]. Ensure the answers are consistent with public communications and reinforce our commitment to resolving the issue."

   - *Example*: "Write an employee FAQ for a financial setback situation, covering common concerns and how the company is addressing them."

3. **Motivational Message for Morale:**

- "Compose a message for employees to boost morale during [specific crisis]. Acknowledge the challenge, appreciate their efforts, and remind them of our collective goals."

- *Example*: "Draft an internal message for the team during a company-wide technical issue, highlighting their hard work and maintaining a positive, hopeful tone."

Apologies and Accountability

1. **Formal Apology Statement:**

- "Draft a formal apology addressing [crisis], taking full accountability and outlining corrective actions. The tone should be sincere, empathetic, and solution-focused."

- *Example*: "Create an apology for a missed deadline that affected clients, stating what went wrong, why it happened, and how we are preventing it in the future."

2. **Customer Communication:**

- "Write a personalized email template for

customers impacted by [issue]. The tone should acknowledge the inconvenience, express sincere apologies, and offer details on compensation or resolution."

- *Example*: "Compose an apology email for customers affected by a service outage, offering compensation details and the timeline for full restoration."

3. **Follow-Up Apology and Progress Update:**

- "Create a follow-up statement that provides an update on the resolution progress of [crisis] after the initial apology. Maintain transparency and reiterate commitment to improvement."

- *Example*: "Draft a follow-up post for social media updating customers on the steps taken since our initial apology for a delayed product launch."

Post-Crisis Reflection and Rebuilding Trust

1. **Sharing Lessons Learned:**

   - "Write a post-crisis report or statement summarizing lessons learned from [specific crisis] and what measures are being implemented to prevent future issues. Ensure the tone is reflective and proactive."

   - *Example*: "Create a LinkedIn article discussing what the company learned from a major supply chain disruption and how it's strengthening future operations."

2. **Customer Assurance Email:**

   - "Draft a reassuring email to customers outlining the long-term changes being made after [crisis]. Emphasize trust and the steps we are taking to reinforce reliability and service quality."

   - *Example*: "Compose an email detailing improvements to our security protocols after a data breach, highlighting why customers can trust our updated processes."

3. **Transparency Report for Stakeholders:**

- "Prepare a transparency report for stakeholders summarizing the timeline and resolution of [crisis]. Include data on response efforts and future strategies."

- *Example*: "Draft a report summarizing our response to a production error, showing data on how quickly we addressed it and improvements made to our QA processes."

Crisis Prevention Communication

1. **Preventative Content:**

- "Create a series of content pieces (e.g., blog posts, social media updates) that outline our proactive measures to avoid [type of crisis]. Keep the tone confident and informative."

- *Example*: "Prepare blog posts explaining our advanced data security measures and training programs to reassure clients and stakeholders."

2. **Webinar or Live Q&A Session:**

- "Develop a script for a live webinar or Q&A session to discuss our approach to managing [type of risk]. Ensure the tone is open and invites questions to build trust."

- *Example*: "Draft a webinar outline discussing our risk management practices in supply chain logistics, sharing examples of strategies we've successfully implemented."

3. **Educational Content on Handling Crises:**

- "Compose an educational LinkedIn post or article sharing tips for other businesses on handling [type of crisis], based on our own experiences and best practices."

- *Example*: "Create a post detailing key takeaways from managing a customer service crisis and steps for other businesses to prepare for similar situations."

Addressing Immediate Operational Issues

1. **Resolving Workflow Bottlenecks:**

   - "Provide instant solutions to resolve a workflow bottleneck in [specific area or process]. Include insights from similar past experiences and highlight actionable steps to implement right away."

   - *Example*: "Offer advice on clearing a bottleneck in the project approval process, based on my experience optimizing workflow for a product development team."

2. **Handling Technical Problems:**

   - "Suggest immediate fixes for [specific technical issue] based on past incidents where I handled similar problems. Include a step-by-step guide for the team to follow."

   - *Example*: "Provide a quick guide for resolving a software bug that is affecting the rollout of a new app feature, using lessons learned from past app development challenges."

3. **Mitigating Missed Deadlines:**

- "Create an action plan to mitigate the impact of a missed deadline for [specific project], using strategies I've employed in the past to manage similar situations."

- *Example*: "Draft a plan to handle a missed product launch deadline, ensuring client communication and internal adjustments are prioritized for minimal disruption."

Client and Stakeholder Issues

1. **Handling Client Concerns:**

- "Compose an immediate response plan for addressing a client's concern about [issue]. Use relevant past interactions where I successfully navigated client issues to inform the solution."

- *Example*: "Provide advice on responding to a client who is concerned about project delays, drawing from experiences in managing client expectations during high-pressure timelines."

2. **Managing Stakeholder Pushback:**

- "Suggest strategies for dealing with stakeholder pushback on [decision or project aspect]. Use examples from times I managed similar conflicts and maintained alignment."

- *Example*: "Write strategies for addressing stakeholder concerns over budget changes mid-project, referencing methods I used to navigate similar challenges."

3. **Responding to Negative Feedback:**

- "Develop a response plan for addressing negative feedback received from a major client. Include steps that align with my past experiences in turning feedback into improvement opportunities."

- *Example*: "Create a plan for responding to negative feedback about service quality, emphasizing acknowledgment, rapid response, and planned improvements."

Team Dynamics and Communication

1. **Resolving Team Conflicts:**

   - "Offer immediate advice for resolving a conflict between team members on [specific issue]. Use strategies I've implemented successfully in past team management scenarios."

   - *Example*: "Draft an approach for addressing a conflict over task ownership within a project team, using insights from managing similar situations effectively."

2. **Boosting Team Morale Under Pressure:**

   - "Suggest instant morale-boosting techniques for the team during [high-stress event or challenge]. Include examples from when I kept team spirits up in similar situations."

   - *Example*: "Provide advice for keeping the team motivated during a tight project deadline, using past methods that balanced productivity with team support."

3. **Improving Communication Gaps:**

- "Develop a quick plan for addressing communication gaps within the team during [specific project phase]. Use proven communication strategies from past projects."

- *Example*: "Compose a plan for improving communication flow during the final review phase of a project, based on past successes in enhancing team collaboration."

Decision-Making Under Pressure

1. **Making Quick Strategic Decisions:**

- "Generate a decision-making framework for [urgent issue or decision] that draws from my past experiences in similar high-stakes situations. Include key factors to consider and potential outcomes."

- *Example*: "Draft a quick decision-making guide for choosing between two potential suppliers when facing supply chain disruptions."

2. **Evaluating Risk Quickly:**

- "Suggest an immediate risk assessment approach for [new challenge] based on how I've managed rapid evaluations in the past. Provide an outline of factors to review and risk mitigation steps."

- *Example*: "Compose a plan for a quick risk assessment when considering adding an unplanned feature to a product launch, referencing previous fast-paced project decisions."

3. **Guiding Real-Time Prioritization:**

- "Develop a priority checklist for tackling [urgent situation] that reflects my approach to triaging tasks and resources during previous high-pressure scenarios."

- *Example*: "Create a prioritization plan for addressing multiple urgent client requests simultaneously, based on past strategies for managing workload peaks."

Crisis Response and Quick Adjustments

1. **Immediate Crisis Handling:**

   - "Draft an emergency response plan for [specific crisis] that leverages my experience in handling past crises. Include immediate steps to control the situation and communicate effectively."

   - *Example*: "Develop a plan for handling a server outage that affects key clients, including immediate communication protocols and temporary solutions."

2. **Adapting to Sudden Changes:**

   - "Provide guidance on how to quickly adapt to [unexpected change, e.g., policy shift or external requirement]. Use examples of how I managed sudden pivots in past projects."

   - *Example*: "Draft a plan for adapting to a new regulatory requirement mid-project, using past experiences with policy changes in regulated industries."

3. **Implementing Quick Fixes:**

- "Suggest quick fixes for [issue, e.g., presentation errors, unexpected data issues], using examples from my experience in fast troubleshooting to prevent major disruptions."

- *Example*: "Write immediate troubleshooting steps for addressing inconsistencies in a client report right before a meeting."

Post-Solution Evaluation

1. **Reviewing the Effectiveness of Quick Solutions:**

- "Create an outline for reviewing the effectiveness of the immediate solutions implemented during [specific situation]. Include lessons learned and improvement for future responses."

- *Example*: "Prepare a post-mortem plan for evaluating how the team handled a last-minute change request, focusing on what went well and what could be improved."

2. **Gathering Team Feedback:**

- "Develop a process for collecting team feedback on how we managed [recent issue].

Ensure it highlights areas for immediate improvement and celebrates successful strategies."

- *Example*: "Compose a plan for gathering team feedback after quickly solving a client's problem, emphasizing open communication and continuous improvement."

3. Documenting Solutions for Future Use:

- "Suggest a framework for documenting quick solutions and their outcomes for [specific problem], making sure it can be easily referenced for future situations."

- *Example*: "Draft a documentation template for recording steps taken during an urgent data recovery incident, outlining what was done and the final result."

Notes

Aaron's story began at age 19, on one of the world's highest mountains, where a life-changing moment taught him the fragility of life and the profound opportunity we all have to make an impact. In an unexpected turn, he saved another man's life, planting the seed of a lifelong mission to inspire and guide others.

As the co-founder of multiple AI startups, Aaron has harnessed cutting-edge technology to help individuals and organizations share their unique stories. With a background as a journalist and podcast host skilled in asking the right questions, he's helped countless people articulate their stories through writing and speaking. His early career in the music industry led to a published book on the business of music, now used in universities, and a speaking career that took him around the globe.

Aaron's work extends beyond music, weaving his expertise into projects with government agencies, sports organizations, not-for-profits, and brands. His initiatives have ranged from creating the Music & Culture Ambassador role for Mississippi to developing strategies with the Gwitchin First Nations to protect the Arctic National Wildlife Refuge.

Through these experiences, Aaron has met leaders, entertainers, and entrepreneurs struggling with imposter syndrome and the search for meaning. His focus is clear: transformation starts from within. By uncovering core stories and aligning them with purpose, Aaron helps individuals and organizations achieve sustainable success and meaningful impact. He believes that **a well-told story not only connects—it creates change.**

To contact Aaron, you can email him at
aaron@aaronbethune.com

www.ingramcontent.com/pod-product-compliance
Lightning Source LLC
LaVergne TN
LVHW011803070326
832902LV00032B/4654